Mur

Retold Myths

The Retold Tales® Series features novels, short story anthologies, and collections of myths and folktales.

Perfection Learning®

Consultants

Angela C. Farris
Kiara Tutorial Center
Atlanta, Georgia

Mildred A. Hill-Lubin
The University of Florida
Gainesville, Florida

Pat McKissick
Author
St. Louis, Missouri

Sandra A. Williams
Southern University
Baton Rouge, Louisiana

Retold Myths & Folktales

African Myths

by Eleanora E. Tate

Perfection Learning®

Editor in Chief
Kathleen Myers

Managing Editor
Beth Obermiller

Senior Editor
Marsha James

Editors
Christine LePorte
Cecelia Munzenmaier
Terry Ofner

Cover and Inside
Illustration
Don Tate II

Book Design
Don Tate II

For information contact
Perfection Learning® Corporation
1000 North Second Avenue, P.O. Box 500
Logan, Iowa 51546-0500
Phone: 1-800-831-4190 • Fax: 1-800-543-2745
perfectionlearning.com

Paperback ISBN 1-5631-2193-x
Cover Craft® ISBN 0-7807-1287-0

ABOUT THE AUTHOR

Eleanora E. Tate

Eleanora E. Tate, a native of Canton, Missouri, has been a professional writer for over 25 years. Her first young adult novel, *Just an Overnight Guest*, was adapted in 1983 into an award-winning movie of the same name.

Her second book, *Secret of Gumbo Grove*, won the Parents' Choice Gold Seal Award in 1987. It was also nominated for a 1991-92 California Young Readers Medal Award.

Ms. Tate has been interested in myths and storytelling for many years. In 1982, she traveled through Europe researching ethnic folktales, and she is the current president of the National Association of Black Storytellers, Inc. Ms. Tate lives in Morehead City, North Carolina.

ABOUT THE ARTIST

Don Tate has been designing and illustrating books and educa-

Don Tate II

tional products for the past 10 years.

Don likes to explore various artistic styles and mediums so that he can match his artistic mood to the mood of the project. Don gained his inspiration for the illustrations in this book by researching African art and sculpture.

Don Tate lives in Des Moines, Iowa. He divides his time between his art projects and his family.

AUTHOR'S PREFACE

The stories in *Retold African Myths* are my literary "inspirations" of age-old tales that have existed for centuries, primarily in oral form. Perfection Learning and its consultants researched and selected the variants which are the basis of the stories in this collection. After this process, the editors invited me to retell the selected versions in my own style and voice.

My objective was not to "improve" the original tales. This would be an impossible goal. Instead, I tried to come to an understanding of the intent and language of the stories in my own way. The result is stories written from unique points of view with a few added characters and situations.

Hopefully, my "inspired" stories will be looked upon as my sincere and humble attempt to pay homage to the legacy of our truly great African myths, folklore, and legends; and to adolescent reading and literacy.

Eleanora E. Tate

TABLE OF CONTENTS

MAP OF AFRICA

WELCOME TO THE RETOLD AFRICAN MYTHS

In Africa, the myths in this book would probably not be read. Rather, they would be told. There is a rich and varied tradition of storytelling in Africa—as rich and varied as the continent of Africa itself. This tradition is full of celebration, humor, and entertainment.

But myths aren't only for entertainment. They also carry on a culture's values from generation to generation. A story about how a heroine faces down a deadly snake helps define strength and goodness. And thrift and generosity are taught when a character creates a disaster through laziness or greed.

The myths in this volume can also serve as a kind of encyclopedia. By reading these myths, you can learn what various cultures think and believe. For example, myths show how early Africans explained the mysteries of life and nature. Why do bats sleep upside down in caves? How did human life begin? Why do people die? The myths in this book provide fascinating answers to such questions.

Finally, these myths are simply great stories. Filled with drama, beauty, and humor, they still attract listeners long after they were first told.

RETOLD UPDATE

This book presents a collection of eighteen adapted myths from the African continent. All the variety, excitement, and humorous details of the original versions are here.

In addition, a word list has been added at the beginning of each story. Each word defined on that list is printed in dark type within the story. If you forget the meaning of one of these words, just check the list to review the definition.

You'll also find footnotes at the bottom of some story

pages. These notes identify people or places, explain ideas, show pronunciations, or provide cultural information.

We offer two other features you may wish to use. One is a map of Africa on the following page. This map locates the region where each of the myths was originally told.

You will also find more cultural information in the Insights sections after each myth. These revealing facts will add to your understanding of the different ways of life in Africa.

One last word. Since many of these myths and stories have been handed down for centuries, several versions exist. So a story you read here will probably differ from a version you read elsewhere.

But that's all part of the tradition. Each storyteller is expected to add something new to the old tales. You may even want to read some of these stories aloud. Adding sound effects and acting out parts will help you come closer to the experience of African storytelling.

The oldest known African myth was first told 2,000 years ago. Now it's your turn to read and retell these timeless stories.

North Atlantic
Ocean
Mediterranean Sea

CANARY ISLANDS

WESTERN
SAHARA

MOROCCO

ALGERIA

TUNISIA

LIBYA

EGYPT

N

MAURITANIA

MALI

NIGER

CHAD

SUDAN

DJIBOUTI

SENEGAL

GAMBIA

GUINEA
BISSAU

② BURKINA
FASO

⑤

SOMALIA

GUINEA

⑦

BENIN

NIGERIA

ETHIOPIA

SIERRA LEONE

IVORY
COAST

⑥

GHANA

TOGO

⑩

CAMEROON

CENTRAL
AFRICAN REPUBLIC

LIBERIA

①

BIOKO

EQUATORIAL GUINEA

GABON

CONGO

ZAIRE

UGANDA

RWANDA

④

KENYA

⑨

Key to Cultural Groups

① Ashanti   ⑦ Mende

② Bambara   ⑧ Sotho

③ Chagga   ⑨ Swahili

④ Ganda   ⑩ Yoruba

⑤ Hausa   ⑪ Zulu

⑥ Kono

BURUNDI

③

TANZANIA

MALAWI

COMOROS

ANGOLA

ZAMBIA

MOZAMBIQUE

MADAGASCAR

ZIMBABWE

South Atlantic Ocean

NAMIBIA

BOTSWANA

SWAZILAND

LESOTHO ⑧

⑪

Indian Ocean

SOUTH AFRICA

CREATION

How Nambi Gained Her Beloved

Obatala Creates the World

Heart Finds a Home

Creation myths are told throughout Africa. Each traditional cultural group tells its own stories of how life began. None of these tales are exactly alike, but they all do one thing. They tell of a supreme god who made the universe.

The Supreme God knows everything. But he is sometimes confusing to humans. For example, he does good things for people, but he can send evil into the world as well.

The Supreme God is known by many different names throughout the continent. In eastern Africa, the Supreme God is usually called Mulungu. Central Africans refer to him as Leza. In the west, he is known as Nyambi. To the Yoruba peoples of Nigeria, the Supreme God is Olorun. You will meet Olorun in the second myth in this section.

HOW NAMBI GAINED HER BELOVED

VOCABULARY PREVIEW

Below is a list of words that appear in the story. Read the list and get to know the words before you read the story.

bore—gave birth to
edible—able to be eaten
ravenous—very hungry
relented—gave in
resourceful—clever; skillful
scornful—critical; doubtful
sustenance—food; nourishment
willful—stubborn

Main Characters

Bee—friend of Nambi
Gulu—sky god
Kaizuki—oldest son of Gulu
Kintu—first man
Nambi—daughter of Gulu
Walumbe—son of Gulu

How Nambi Gained Her Beloved

Adapted from a tale of Uganda

Gods and humans usually kept their distance—that is, until Kintu and Nambi fell in love. While Kintu was only a man, Nambi was the daughter of the great sky god. Could a bee help Kintu pass the sky god's tests so that the two lovers could be united?

In the first days, the goddess Nambi[1] lived in heaven. She lived there with her father, Gulu,[2] the sky god. Her two brothers— Walumbe and Kaizuki[3]—lived in heaven as well.

[1] (nam´ bē)
[2] (gu´ lu)
[3] (wal um´ bā) (ka ē zu´ kē)

One day Nambi decided to visit earth. Now Nambi was sometimes **willful** and independent. So Gulu sent her brother Walumbe to watch after her.

Soon after Nambi and Walumbe stepped on earth, they came upon a man sleeping beside his cow. The sleeper was Kintu,[4] the first man. The cow was the First Mother of **Sustenance.** The cow gave Kintu all that he needed to eat.

Upon seeing the man, Nambi fell in love with him. But her brother Walumbe was **scornful.** "You have been made crazy by the sun's blazing rays," he said. "This man has no wealth. Notice, he sleeps on the ground, so he must have no dwelling. His only companion is this cow, so she probably feeds him. Must a lowly cowherd become the husband of the royal daughter of the heavens?"

"Hush up," Nambi said. "And quit talking about his cow."

Nambi woke the man and introduced herself. "I'm Nambi, daughter of the sky god. I want to marry you."

Nambi saw Walumbe frown and added quickly, "But first you must be accepted by my father and my brothers. If you agree, I will come back for you soon."

"I would be honored," replied Kintu with surprise in his voice.

Walumbe fussed all the way home. How could his sister want to marry a human!

Upon their return to heaven, Nambi and Walumbe went to their father, King Gulu. Walumbe was first to speak.

"Nambi wants to marry the first earth man she sees!" he complained. "This marriage would cause us all shame."

King Gulu thought about the problem for a moment. Then he made a decision. "We'll test the man three times," Gulu said to Nambi. "If he passes the tests, I'll let you marry him."

Walumbe came up with the first test. "I want to see how long Kintu can live without his cow," he said to Gulu and Nambi. "I will hide the cow in the royal herd."

And so Walumbe returned to earth and stole Kintu's cow. He hid it in Gulu's royal herd in heaven.

---

[4] (kin´ tu)

Nambi watched from above while Kintu searched for the missing cow. With no milk to drink or cheese to eat, he soon grew **ravenous.** Nambi decided to help her beloved. So she sent a friendly bee from the royal pasture down to earth.

But when Kintu spied the bee, he tried to kill it for food. "You haven't been in the habit of eating living things," Bee said. "You don't have to start with me. There's plenty of food all around you. Follow me."

The bee flew about and showed Kintu the plants he could eat. In this way humans first learned about **edible** plants. And Kintu was able to live without his cow. So he passed his first test.

Gulu was impressed. "Your man is very **resourceful,**" he told Nambi. "You may return to earth and bring Kintu to heaven for a visit."

Walumbe was disappointed that Kintu had passed the first test. "But he won't pass the next one!" he told himself.

Walumbe was the first to greet Nambi and Kintu when they returned to heaven. "Welcome," Walumbe told Kintu with a smile. "In your behalf, our servants have prepared a feast for you."

Then Walumbe led Kintu into a large room. Kintu was surprised to see tables covered with breads, vegetables, and fruits of all kinds.

"This must be another test," Nambi whispered to Kintu. "Walumbe will watch to see if you can eat all the food. If not, the wedding will be called off."

Walumbe smiled again and made his sister leave the room. Then he locked the door. Kintu was left to eat all the food by himself.

Kintu ate and ate and ate, but there was still food left. After much worrying, he thought to pull back the mat on the floor. Seeing a loose board, he quickly pulled it up. There was space below. Kintu dropped all the food into the hole and replaced the board.

King Gulu and Nambi's other brother, Kaizuki, were pleased when they saw Kintu seated at the empty table. Walumbe, however, was furious. He persuaded Gulu and

Kaizuki to let him put Kintu to the third and last test.

"See this rock?" said Walumbe, holding up a large stone. "Our father requires special fuel for his fires. Chop fuel from this rock."

"Walumbe, you're being very unfair," Nambi said.

Gulu interrupted. "The man who becomes your husband will have to be extra smart. You see who he'll have to put up with!"

Nambi **relented** and sadly led Kintu away. She was sure Kintu would fail the last test. But Kintu was not ready to give up.

Taking an ax, Kintu wedged the blade into tiny cracks in the rock. Patiently he wiggled the blade back and forth. Rock chips finally fell to the ground. Kintu then mixed the chips with tree bark.

"I have brought you fuel for your fire," Kintu said respectfully to Gulu. And when Kintu tossed the rock and bark into Gulu's royal fire, flames burst up.

Nambi and Kaizuki applauded. "Kintu, you have my blessing and my daughter," Gulu said.

"But wait," Walumbe said in a loud voice. "Don't forget your cow, Kintu. You wouldn't want to return to earth without her, would you?"

"I was about to discuss the sacredness of marriage, Walumbe," Gulu said. "Can't the cow wait?"

"Let's take care of this small matter first," Walumbe said quickly.

"There he goes again," Nambi whispered. "All of those cows look alike. If you choose the wrong one, you'll look foolish. Walumbe will persuade my father to not let us wed."

But Kintu was not left helpless. As Walumbe led him to the royal pasture, the friendly bee lit on Kintu's ear. "Watch me carefully," Bee said. "I'll show you which one is your cow. Then I'll show you her new calves too."

Kintu watched the bee as the first herd of cows was paraded by. But Bee didn't move. "My cow isn't in this herd," Kintu said confidently.

Kintu again shook his head as the second herd was led by.

But when the third herd walked by, Bee lit on a cow's tail. "This is my cow," Kintu declared. Bee went on to light on two small calves. "And these are her calves that she **bore** while here."

"You are indeed a smart man," said Gulu with admiration. "You may marry my daughter. Welcome to the family!"

So Nambi and Kintu were wed and left that day to start their new life on earth.

This is how the first man and first woman came into the world. This is also why people and bees are good friends and live in harmony.

As for Walumbe, he lived to create more problems for Kintu and Nambi. Perhaps someday you will hear more of the story.

INSIGHTS

The story of Kintu and Nambi is part of an epic told in Buganda—one of the regions of Uganda in central Africa. This epic tells of the brave deeds of Kintu, the founder of Buganda.

Most epics are based on actual people and events. But as the story is retold, the human characters can become almost godlike. That is what happened to Kintu.

In the Buganda epic, Kintu was the first man. In history he was the first king of Uganda.

Before the historical Kintu was born, the tribes in Uganda were small and scattered. Kintu gathered them into one nation. People respected him so much that they said he was descended from the gods.

According to tradition, King Kintu didn't have a wife. The god Gulu saw that the king was lonely. So Gulu gave Kintu his own daughter—Nambi.

After Kintu died, the legend of his many deeds lived on. All the kings of Uganda claim they are related to the great Kintu.

OBATALA CREATES THE WORLD

VOCABULARY PREVIEW

Below is a list of words that appear in the story. Read the list and get to know the words before you read the story.

consult—talk with; ask for advice
descent—downward movement
disfigured—deformed; imperfect
domain—land belonging to a ruler
potential—possibilities; promise
thatched—covered with leaves or other plant materials

Main Characters

Chameleon—messenger for the Supreme God
Obatala—god who made humans
Olokun—goddess of the marshes
Olorun—Supreme God
Orunmila—god who knows the future; Olorun's son

*When the heavens were made, the earth didn't
exist. Most of the gods were content with this
plan. But young Obatala was bored. He wanted
things to be different. So he set out to find what
he could make.*

OBATALA CREATES THE WORLD

Adapted from a Yoruba tale

In the beginning of Yoruba Time, all things
waited to be made or improved upon. There was
heaven—where the gods lived—and water below
it. But there was no solid ground. No sun shone
down upon the mists. And there were no people
to laugh or work below the sky.

The goddess Olokun[1] ruled the grayness
hanging between the water and heaven. All the
mists and marshes belonged to her. She liked
things the way they were in her **domain.**

But Obatala[2]—one of the younger gods—
thought things were too empty. All those mists
and gray clouds bored Obatala. So the young god

[1] (ōl´ ō kun)
[2] (ōb a tal´ a)

formed a plan. Then he went to talk to the Supreme God, Olorun.[3]

It was Olorun who ruled the sky and all the other gods and goddesses. He too was satisfied with things as they were.

But the Supreme God had a soft spot for the energetic Obatala. In fact, the two gods could have been father and son—they were that close. So when Obatala begged to speak to Olorun, the Supreme God listened.

Obatala eagerly began explaining his idea. "If I had my way, I could do some wonderful things with Olokun's marshes and swamps," he announced. "I could create solid land down there, with dry fields and forests.

"Just think," he continued enthusiastically, "we could all live down there! It would be a great thing for us. Goddess Olokun simply doesn't realize the **potential** of what she has."

The Supreme God smiled at Obatala. "As always, Obatala, you're full of interesting ideas."

"I have your permission then?" Obatala asked quickly.

Olorun nodded. "You may begin," he said. "But first talk to my son Orunmila.[4] He can help you. Tell him that I sent you."

Now the god Orunmila was a wise diviner.[5] The future held no secrets from him, and he knew the mystery of all things.

Obatala went immediately to **consult** Orunmila about his plan. Orunmila let the excited younger god talk himself out.

After Obatala was finished, the diviner said, "You'll need to make a chain of gold. This chain must reach from the sky down to the waters."

"A chain of gold," Obatala repeated excitedly. "What else?"

"Fill a snail shell with sand. Then find a white hen, a black cat, and a palm nut. Put all of these things in a bag. When you climb down the golden chain, take the bag with you."

[3] (ōl´ ōr un)
[4] (ōr un mil´ a)
[5] A diviner is a person who tells the future. Diviners are still a part of Yoruba culture.

Obatala thanked Orunmila and left to round up all the gold he could find. He took it to the goldsmith, who just shook his head. "You'll hang in the air for a long time if this is all the gold you have," the goldsmith warned.

"It's the best I could do," Obatala told him. "Do what you can with what I gave you. And please be sure to put a hook at one end of the chain."

When the goldsmith finished his work, Obatala and Orunmila went to the end of the sky. There Obatala fastened the hook of the chain to the sky's edge.

Next, Obatala wrapped the bag around his wrist. Then saying farewell to Orunmila, the young god gripped the chain and began his **descent.**

Time passed. As Obatala climbed lower, the light dimmed. Finally it got so gray he couldn't see a thing. But he could hear waves as they crashed against each other in the sea below. Then Obatala came to the end of the chain.

"I may be a god, but I can't swim," Obatala thought as he dangled from the chain. He hung there for a long time, thinking and worrying. Then, from far above, Obatala heard Orunmila's voice.

"What did you say?" he shouted back.

"The sand," Orunmila called down. "Pour the sand from the shell into the water."

"What good will that do?" Obatala hollered back.

"Just do what I say," Orunmila told him.

Obatala obeyed.

"Now the hen," said Orunmila.

"The hen?" thought Obatala. He opened his mouth to argue. But his arms were getting tired. Maybe it was a crazy idea, but it was better than falling into the sea.

"The hen," commanded Orunmila. "Free the white hen!"

Obatala pulled the hen from the bag. With a cluck and a flutter, the hen flapped down to the water. She scratched at the sand with her feet, scattering the sand in all directions. And wherever the sand fell, hills and valleys formed.

Obatala let go of the chain and fell to the new land. Earth stretched everywhere. There was promise of more new things to come.

The young god's first action was to plant the palm nut. Immediately a palm tree sprang up and quickly grew to its full height.

Next Obatala used the bark of the palm to build a small house. He then **thatched** a roof for his house using the tree's leaves. Obatala stood back and admired his work.

"I name this place Ife, meaning 'wide,' and Ile,[6] meaning 'house,'" Obatala said.

This is how Ile-Ife, the most sacred city of the Yoruba people, came to be.

After some time had passed, the Supreme God Olorun sent his messenger, Chameleon, down to check on Obatala.

Chameleons, as you know, take on the color of whatever object they are near. So as soon as Chameleon touched the chain, he turned a golden color. He sparkled and glittered during his long descent to Ile-Ife.

Obatala noticed the bright glitter coming toward him. He soon recognized Chameleon and invited the messenger into his home.

Chameleon sat on the grass mat. He immediately turned a brilliant emerald green.

"The Great Olorun sent me," said Chameleon. "He wants to know how you are doing."

"As you can see, we have a fine beginning," Obatala told him. "But it is awfully gray down here. Could you ask the Great Olorun to make it brighter?"

Chameleon returned to Olorun with Obatala's request. The Supreme God immediately created the sun and rolled it across the sky. Ile-Ife was bathed in warm, golden light.

With the creation of the sun, all was well in Ile-Ife. All was well except that Obatala was lonely. He needed someone to talk to. Therefore he decided to create beings who could share his new world.

Obatala didn't have much to work with. So he began cre-

---

[6] (ē´ fay) (ē´ lay) Ife is a city in western Nigeria.

ating tiny figures out of mud. He shaped figures who looked a good deal like himself.

But Obatala's work made him thirsty. He took a break to drink some wine made from palm juice. Unfortunately the wine made his brain and fingers clumsy. When he returned to work, several pieces slipped from his hands and became **disfigured.**

Obatala laid his figures in the sun to dry. But he didn't notice the misshapen people. When he finished, he called to the Supreme God. "Great Olorun, only you can breathe life into what I have made. If they are pleasing to you, bring my people to life."

Instantly Obatala's creations changed into real people.

Happy with his work, Obatala found his way to his house. There he slept off the palm wine.

When Obatala awoke, he was alarmed to find several imperfect people. One that fell on his leg had a bent leg. One that fell on his head spent all his time thinking.

Looking at them made the god sorrowful. From that day, he vowed never to touch wine again. Obatala also became the protector of all people born with imperfections.

This is how all life came to be.

INSIGHTS

The Yoruba people have a long history dating back to around 300 B.C. At that time they developed several city-states near the Niger River. About ten million Yoruba still live in this area of Nigeria.

Today, many Yoruba follow the Christian or Muslim religions. But believers in the traditional Yoruba ways say they are descended from Orunmila, the diviner. A diviner is someone who foretells the future. As in the myth, a Yoruba diviner usually doesn't make detailed predictions. Rather, he suggests the best way to act or warns against dangers. His advice helps people understand the will of the gods.

Many Yoruba households have a shrine to this god, who is also known as the god of knowledge.

In the myth, a goldsmith makes Obatala's chain for him. This goldsmith is actually Ogun, the god of iron.

Ogun is still worshipped by the Yoruba—especially anyone who works with metal. In fact, some truck drivers always pray to Ogun before a trip. Otherwise, they believe Ogun might cause an accident while they are driving.

We saw in the myth how Obatala was able to form human beings from clay. However, only the Supreme God Olorun was able to breathe life into Obatala's clay forms.

Obatala was jealous of Olorun's life-giving power. He was determined to discover Olorun's secret. So one night he hid near some of his human forms to see Olorun at work.

But Olorun knew everything—including Obatala's plan. So before going to work, he put Obatala into a deep sleep. As a result, Obatala never did discover the secret of life.

HEART FINDS A HOME

VOCABULARY PREVIEW

Below is a list of words that appear in the story. Read the list and get to know the words before you read the story.

abode—home; dwelling
agitated—troubled; disturbed
compassion—feeling of tenderness and concern
marveled—wondered; was in awe
mulled—thought over
pledges—promises

Main Characters

High God—creator of all things
First Man
First Woman
Moon   —children of the High God
Night
Rain
Sun
Mutima—Heart

The creator made the world and then went away. Left behind, Mutima was lonely. He searched for the High God until he found an answer to the longing in his heart.

HEART FINDS A HOME

ADAPTED FROM A TALE OF UGANDA

In the earliest of times, God created Earth, Sun, Moon, Night, and Rain. Then God came to Earth and made the First Man and the First Woman.

God didn't stay with his creation long. Soon after all was made, God prepared to return to heaven. But before he left, he created Heart and named him Mutima.[1]

Now Mutima **marveled**

[1] (mu tē´ ma)

at all that the highest god had created. The more he marveled, the more he wished he could meet the creator of such wonders. So one day, Mutima went walking in search of the Most High God.

Along the way, Mutima met Rain. He introduced himself.

"I'm looking for the Most High God," said Mutima. "Have you seen him?"

"I haven't seen him for ages," replied Rain.

This news **agitated** Mutima. "Where has God gone?" he asked. "What are we to do without him?"

"His absence makes no difference to me," replied Rain. "I'll just rain until it floods."

"Have mercy," cried Mutima. "Listen, let Sun dry out the land a bit before you rain again. Use a balanced hand."

Rain **mulled** this over and decided that this was good. Mutima and Rain became friends.

Mutima next met Sun. He introduced himself.

"Have you seen the Most High God?" he asked. "I would like to meet him."

"You won't find him around here," replied Sun. "I think he withdrew to heaven."

"Oh, no!" cried Mutima. "What are we to do without him?"

Sun replied, "I hadn't thought much about doing anything else except shine and burn, shine and burn."

"Have pity," said Mutima, with **compassion.** "The people's crops will shrivel up. Listen, after you've warmed the Earth, please give Rain a chance to refresh things a little."

Sun considered Mutima's plea and decided that it was good. They became friends.

Mutima then met Night and Moon and introduced himself to them. He asked Night if she had seen the Most High God.

"He has gone to heaven," Night answered. "His **abode** is farther away than the farthest star."

"This is terrible," said Mutima. "What are we to do?"

"I don't know about you, but it's no problem for me," said Night.

"Why?" asked Mutima. "What are your plans?"

"To keep everything dark, of course."

"Oh, have a heart," said Mutima. "Man and Woman will never see the beautiful Earth that God has created. Night, try this. Share time with Sun and Moon. There's enough room for everyone."

Night thought this over and decided that it was good. Moon was pleased as well. They all became friends.

Sun, Night, Moon, and Rain held to their **pledges.** Night and Moon made their rounds and made room for Sun. After Sun warmed the earth, Rain brought refreshment.

Mutima was glad that he had met the other children of the High God. But he still longed to meet God himself.

Mutima continued walking. Then Mutima saw the First Man and the First Woman planting crops in a field.

"I cannot find God," Mutima said. "But I've found his children."

Opening wide his arms, Mutima greeted the man and woman. He decided to share his heart with them until God came back.

Mutima still lives with the people. And that's why all men and women have compassion. And that's why all people share Mutima's longing for God's return.

INSIGHTS

The story about Mutima, or Heart, is from the Ganda people. The Ganda once ruled the largest kingdom in Africa. Today they are the main cultural group in Uganda. Nearly one million Ganda live northwest of Lake Victoria. Their official religion is Christianity.

As in this story, many African myths tell that the creator once lived on earth. But for one reason or another, he left to live in heaven.

A Mende tradition says that the creator lived on earth with the first people. He allowed the people to ask him for whatever they needed. When they asked for something, he would reply, "Just take it." This happened so often that people thought God's name was "Just Take It."

Finally, the creator got tired of the people's constant demands. So he left to find a place where he wouldn't be bothered.

Another African story tells of a woman who was grinding corn into flour. She was using a club with a long handle. Because of her carelessness, the handle of the club hit the High God in the eye. He got angry and left to find a more peaceful place.

One story says the sky was so close to the earth that people could touch it. At first the High God lived in the sky close to the people. But he left when people started using his beard for a towel.

DEATH

Death and the River King

Walumbe's Revenge

Why Folks Must Die

All cultures have an explanation of why people die and what happens to them after death. In many African myths, the first men and women were to live forever. But then death came into the world because of a mistake or an accident.

The myths in this section give three versions of how death came to live here on earth.

DEATH AND THE RIVER KING

VOCABULARY PREVIEW

Below is a list of words that appear in the story. Read the list and get to know the words before you read the story.

barbs—insults
eternal—never-ending
miserable—poor
protruding—sticking out of the surface of an object
regal—kingly; dignified; noble
rivalry—competition
trespass—enter; intrude

Main Characters

Death
Hunter
Tano—river god

There once was a man who was a terrible hunter. One day he came upon an antelope. Taking a deep breath, he let fly his best shot. Little did the man know that his fateful arrow would bring death into the world.

DEATH
AND THE RIVER KING

Inspired by a tale from the people of Togo

There was once a man who was a terrible hunter. He rarely found game. When he did, he lost the tracks and the animal escaped.

Since the man's aim was as bad as his tracking, he rarely hit anything. You see, when he shot arrows to the left, they flew off to the right. When he shot to the right, they flew off to the left.

One morning the man saw an antelope drinking from the river near his village. He was so excited, he almost dropped his bow. But he took a deep breath and let fly his best shot.

The hunter had aimed to the left, so of course, his arrow sailed off to the right. But listen! The antelope bounded away—to the right! And the man's arrow actually plunged into the antelope's side!

The antelope sped away, leaping into a clump of bushes along the riverbank. The happy hunter jumped after the antelope. Thump! He landed in a clearing.

What he saw there filled him with amazement and fear. He found no antelope. Instead he beheld the mighty river god Tano.[1] And an arrow was **protruding** from his thigh.

The frightened man fell to his knees. "Oh, my Lord, I beg your mercy!" he cried. "I didn't know it was you. Oh, please, forgive me. I'll never hunt again."

Tano pulled the arrow from his thigh. "I've watched your **miserable** hunting for many years. How you were able to shoot me, neither of us will ever understand. Stand up, hunter. I'm not harmed."

The man, however, stayed on his knees. He begged and begged Tano's pardon. Then to show his complete goodwill, the hunter invited Tano to his home.

"I only have a simple meal of bread, fruit, and yams," the hunter said. "But you're welcome to all I have."

Tano was touched by the invitation and accepted. But just as Tano and the hunter turned toward the man's home, up jumped Death.

"And where do you go, River God?" Death asked in a firm voice.

"To visit my new friend, if you must know," Tano replied.

"But to do that, you must cross over *my* land," said Death. "You can't do that without my permission. You may rule the water, but I rule the land."

You see, Death and Tano had a long-standing **rivalry**. Death was in charge of the land, while Tano controlled the

[1] (ta′ nō)

water. But each one was always trying to **trespass** on the other's territory.

"You have no authority to order us around," Tano declared. "We go where we please."

Death held up his hand in a warning. "You should keep me happy. I have ways of getting what I want. You may not step on my land without my permission. And *I* don't give permission!"

Tano hesitated. Then he sat down on a log to think over his enemy's words. But shortly he stood up and faced Death.

> My name is Tano, River King,
> And I go wherever I please.
> You got about as much rule over me
> As a hyena[2] has over its fleas.

Death frowned up at Tano. He crossed his arms and stroked his chin. Just as Tano and the hunter started past him again, Death shouted,

> Stop! You may be Tano and you may be king.
> But with Brother Death, that don't mean a thing.
> The land is mine; you better do as I say.
> With Death in charge, there's no other way.

Tano cut in,

> You talk up a streak,
> But your words are cheap.
> Move out of the way;
> I got appointments to keep.

And so it went back and forth, each one stopping the other with words. They kept it up for two days and two nights. Finally Tano and Death ran out of insults and comebacks. The two gods sat in silence, searching their memories for fresh **barbs.**

---

[2] A hyena is a large doglike mammal.

Finally the hunter got up and said in a tired voice, "You two go ahead. I'm heading home to get something to eat."

"Okay, okay!" said Death. "Let's try this. Whoever reaches the hunter's home first can be his guest for dinner and spend the night."

Tano quickly agreed. He and the hunter went one way. Death went another.

Being ruler over the land, Death was convinced he could reach the hunter's hut first. But the hunter knew of a shortcut, so he and his **regal** guest arrived first.

Tano was waiting at the entrance of the hunter's compound[3] when Death ran up, all out of breath. With a playful smile, Tano poked fun at Death. "What, did you get lost on the way? Some king of the land you make."

Death ran away in a huff, and Tano claimed the hunter's friendship and his dinner. He also got to spend the night.

Now if this had been the end of it, Tano would have been the winner. And people would never have died.

But being a sneak, Death crept back while the hunter lay in bed. He took the only thing that Tano didn't claim: the hunter's sleep.

Even so, Death didn't get things all his own way. Thanks to Tano, Death couldn't claim the hunter's life until the man grew old.

This is why death sneaks up on people when they are least aware. This is also why death is sometimes called the "**eternal sleep.**"

---

[3] A compound is an enclosed living area that contains several dwellings.

INSIGHTS

Tano is one of the most important gods of the country of Togo in western Africa. He is a son of the Supreme God Nyamia. Tano is also honored as the creator of human beings. But he is perhaps best known as the god of the Tano River and the fertile lands through which it flows. However, Tano wasn't always ruler of this important river. Indeed, he had to trick his father to gain control of his river.

It seems that Nyamia thought that Tano was too disobedient to rule over the river. So the Supreme God was going to grant the river to his oldest son, Bia. He planned to give the barren and less fruitful places to Tano.

But Nyamia made the mistake of telling his plan to Goat, who was Tano's friend. Goat advised Tano to disguise himself as Bia and get to Nyamia's house early the next morning. Then Goat told Bia to take his time.

Tano did as Goat advised. Sure enough, Tano's disguise fooled his father. Without realizing it, Nyamia named Tano ruler of the fertile lands.

Bia angrily demanded his rights. But since Nyamia's word was law, it was too late to change his decision. Bia had to settle for second best.

"Death and the River King" explains why death sneaks up on people. But according to some African people, death doesn't always come as a surprise.

Some people of central Zaire believe that there are signs that a person is about to die. For example, a villager certainly wouldn't want to meet a young person with glowing eyes during a walk in the bush. This is a sign that the villager will die that night.

WALUMBE'S REVENGE

VOCABULARY PREVIEW

Below is a list of words that appear in the story. Read the list and get to know the words before you read the story.

commotion—fuss; noisy confusion
confront—challenge; stand up to
mortal—human being
outraged—offended; angry
possessive—controlling; selfish; stingy

Main Characters

Gulu—sky god
Kaizuki—oldest son of Gulu
Kintu—first man; husband of Nambi
Nambi—first woman; daughter of Gulu; wife of Kintu
Walumbe—son of Gulu

Walumbe, the youngest son of the sky god, was angry at his sister for marrying a human. But Walumbe found a way to get back at her. And his revenge is with us still.

WALUMBE'S REVENGE*

Adapted from a tale of Uganda

This is how Death came to live here on earth.

Kintu[1]—the first man—and Nambi[2]—the first woman—got married in heaven. Nambi was the daughter of the sky god, Gulu.[3] He was happy for the couple. So was Nambi's brother, Kaizuki.[4] Both Gulu and Kaizuki attended the wedding and brought many gifts.

However, Walumbe[5]—Nambi's other brother—didn't attend the celebration.

---

* See "How Nambi Gained Her Beloved," pp. 3-9.
[1] (kin´ tu)
[2] (nam´ bē)
[3] (gu´ lu)
[4] (ka ē zu´ kē)
[5] (wal um´ bā)

He was very **possessive** of his royal sister and didn't want to let her go. He especially didn't want her to marry an ordinary **mortal** like Kintu. In fact, he had tried every trick he knew to prevent the wedding.

But despite Walumbe's tricks, Nambi became Kintu's bride. Then the couple prepared for the journey to earth. Nambi gathered her royal goats, sheep, and chickens while Kintu gathered his cows and his friend, the bee.

Before the couple left heaven, they went to say good-bye to Nambi's father. But as they prepared to go, Gulu gave the couple a warning. "Once you leave heaven, don't return," Gulu said sternly. "If you do, Walumbe will find you out and follow you to earth. There's no telling what tricks Walumbe might pull to get revenge."

Nambi thanked her father, and the couple started on their journey.

But after the couple had gone a short distance, Nambi's chickens began to fuss. They were hungry. However, being royalty, they refused to eat common seeds from the ground. They must have *royal* corn fed to them from their *royal* bowls. So they clucked, squawked, flapped their wings, and raised a **commotion** that could be heard for miles.

Such noise put Kintu and Nambi in great danger.

"Can't you keep your chickens quiet?" Kintu said. "Walumbe is sure to hear this noise and find us."

But Nambi's chickens continued to complain. Finally Nambi and Kintu decided to go back for the royal corn.

Gulu scolded the couple when he found that they had returned to heaven. "I told you not to ever come back here!" Gulu said with alarm. "Now Walumbe will surely find you."

Gulu hastily gave them the corn and told them to hurry away before Walumbe saw them.

The two left quickly. But just as Kintu and Nambi slipped out of heaven, Walumbe spied them. Unnoticed, he followed them to earth.

One day Walumbe appeared before the couple, hungry and tired of living alone. He asked his sister for some food.

Kintu was **outraged** when he saw Walumbe. "He isn't

welcome in our house," he told Nambi. "Keep him away from here."

Nambi tried her best to keep her brother away. But now that he knew where they lived, there was really nothing she could do.

As time passed, Nambi and Kintu became the parents of many children. Indeed, a comfortable village grew up around their house.

Of course, Walumbe was not allowed in the village. But when he saw how happy Kintu and Nambi were, he became jealous.

One day while Nambi was gone, Walumbe stood outside their house and called to Kintu. "I have no children to help me," Walumbe complained. "Could I borrow one or two of yours to help harvest my fields?"

"I've seen how you beat and starve your animals," Kintu told Walumbe. "I'll never even let you touch my children!"

"Unlike your chickens, your children aren't royalty," Walumbe shouted back. "Give me a child or you'll be sorry!"

"Never!"

The next morning Kintu's eldest son burned with fever. By sunset he was dead. Everybody grieved and wailed at the boy's funeral. Everybody but Walumbe, that is.

The next day another of Kintu's children fell ill and died, and then another.

Other children died. Then grown-ups began to die. Kintu believed that Walumbe was causing this sorrow. So he went to his father-in-law for help.

Gulu shook his head. "Remember how I warned you not to return to heaven? You and your people would have been protected against Walumbe and his deadly ways. But now he has followed you and knows where you live.

"I have only one suggestion," Gulu continued. "Maybe Nambi's older brother can do something to stop him. Kaizuki is the only one who ever stood up to Walumbe."

So Kintu went to Kaizuki with his problem. Kaizuki agreed to talk to Walumbe.

The next day Kaizuki appeared at Walumbe's door. "What good does it do to kill people?" Kaizuki asked his younger brother. "If you keep on killing, people will pay attention to you. But they won't serve you. And though they fear you, they'll never love you.

You're hurting them without gaining anything for yourself."

But Walumbe was angry and he was stubborn. He just kept on killing.

Kaizuki was afraid that death would claim more and more people until no one was left alive. But Walumbe still refused to listen to him. So Kaizuki was forced to **confront** Walumbe, and the two brothers fought.

Kaizuki was the stronger of the two, and he easily threw his brother to the ground. Walumbe quickly understood that he couldn't win in a fair fight. So he ran from his brother and disappeared into a hole near the town's goat pasture.

The villagers cheered when Kaizuki returned from the fight. But Kaizuki knew that Walumbe wasn't defeated. He told the townspeople to keep their children safely at home. Then he took a few brave men. They hid near the pasture and waited for Walumbe.

Meanwhile Walumbe got lonely hiding from everyone. So he sneaked out of his hole. He hoped that no one would notice him walking around.

Walumbe walked until he came to the goat pasture. But as he approached, the goats began bleating and making a terrible noise. For when Walumbe approached, they smelled Death.

Kaizuki heard the noise and rushed from his hiding place. But Walumbe saw him and disappeared again.

Walumbe made his home under the ground. He continued to hide and he continued to kill. Every so often, a child would die or an elder would not wake up. Everyone knew that Walumbe was at it again—he had taken more people to his underground home.

Kaizuki kept trying to find Walumbe to stop his killing. But Death—as Walumbe came to be called—always managed to escape. Finally Kaizuki got discouraged and returned to heaven.

Death, however, remains on earth, taking people back to his home whenever he gets lonely. He hasn't been captured yet.

INSIGHTS

This myth continues the Buganda story of the first man and woman. It is part of the epic of Kintu and Nambi. Because this epic has been told so many times, many versions of this myth exist. Sometimes Nambi is the one who returns for the corn. Sometimes it is Kintu who disobeys Gulu. But in all versions, Gulu tells the first people that because they returned to heaven, they have to die.

In "Walumbe's Revenge," people die because one of the first people made a mistake. The idea that people's foolishness caused death is common in other African stories as well.

In Zambia, the Ila say that the first man and woman were given a choice. The High God asked them to pick one of two bags. They selected the brighter sack, which contained death.

Feeling sorry for the couple, the creator gave them a second chance. If they were able to resist eating for a certain period of time, they would live forever. But the people ate before the time was up. The first man and woman never got another chance to live forever.

WHY FOLKS MUST DIE

VOCABULARY PREVIEW

Below is a list of words that appear in the story. Read the list and get to know the words before you read the story.

aggravated—angry
contemplate—think about carefully
fowl—bird
incompetent—unfit; unable
longevity—life span; length of life
malicious—cruel; mean
meddle—snoop; stick one's nose in
sneered—scoffed; talked down

Main Characters

Chameleon—messenger for the Supreme God
Monkey—messenger for the Supreme God
Unkulunkulu—Supreme God

WHY FOLKS MUST DIE

Inspired by a tale from the Zulu people

Chameleon was so proud to be chosen as the High God's messenger. Was it really his fault that people must die?

In the beginning, men and women lived for a very, very long time. In fact, they lived as long as trees. Now the Supreme God Unkulunkulu[1] approved of people living so long. In fact, he wanted to give them even greater **longevity.**

So Unkulunkulu decided to send the people a message. This message would let the people know that they would live forever.

"Send for Old Chameleon," Unkulunkulu told his servant. "Tell him that I

[1] (un´ ku lun´ ku lu)

have an important message that only he can carry."

The servant went in search of Old Chameleon. However, he learned that the lizard was out of town. So he sent for Old Chameleon's grandson instead.

Now chameleons are known for being smart. They are also known for being slow. But this particular chameleon, while extremely slow, was not very smart.

After several months, the young chameleon reached Unkulunkulu. The Great God was **aggravated** at the delay. "A man could grow old waiting for you to move from one place to another," he said angrily.

"Listen closely, Chameleon," Unkulunkulu continued in a stern voice. "You will be my messenger. Tell people that I have a gift for them. Tell them that people will never die and that they will live as long as gods. And Chameleon?"

"Yes, your majesty," replied the young lizard.

"You must hurry," ordered Unkulunkulu. "You have already let too much time go by."

The young chameleon's throat swelled with pride at this important task. He turned as red as the royal clay tile he sat upon. Then he crawled outside to **contemplate** this wonderful assignment.

Just as he stepped outside, Chameleon spied Monkey near the palace. "The Great Unkulunkulu has chosen me to give a message to the people," he bragged. "I take the place of my grandfather for this mission."

"Congratulations," Monkey said politely. "It's always good when our young folks can be of service to the Great God."

But after Chameleon left, Monkey went straight inside to complain to Unkulunkulu. "I happened to see a young chameleon leave your palace," he said to the Great God. "You thought his grandfather was slow? This one hasn't even gotten past the royal grounds. But maybe you're not in any hurry to tell folks anything.

"Not that it's any of my business," Monkey added as if he didn't care. "But I thought you ought to know."

Unkulunkulu was irritated to have Monkey **meddle** in his

business. But he was even more irritated to find that his servant had chosen an **incompetent** messenger.

"Then, Monkey, you shall take a message too. The message that reaches the people first will become the law. Tell folks that they are *not* like gods. They must die. In fact, people will not even live as long as trees."

Monkey rushed away with Unkulunkulu's message. As he left, he passed Chameleon. "See you around," **sneered** Monkey. "You can't crawl any faster than a yam can grow. And you're no smarter than a yam either."

Slow-moving Chameleon thought about these **malicious** words for several days. Finally he decided to put them out of his mind. After all, he needed to concentrate on his duty. His grandfather would be very proud of the message he carried for Unkulunkulu.

Monkey, meanwhile, told everyone he saw—human, fish, and **fowl**—that they all must die. "And no, you're not like gods," Monkey said. "People won't even live as long as trees. Unkulunkulu told me this himself."

Several months later, Chameleon finally reached a group of men and women working in a field. Puffing himself up, he delivered his message. "The Great Unkulunkulu gives this gift to all people," he said. "All men and women will never die! Unkulunkulu says that people will live as long as gods. People will live even longer than trees."

But no one listened to Chameleon. In fact, they acted as if they didn't even hear him.

This wasn't the reaction he'd expected. Puzzled, Chameleon cleared his throat and repeated his message.

"Don't we wish," one of the people replied.

"What do you mean?" asked Chameleon.

"Monkey brought a message from the Great Unkulunkulu last spring," a man said. "Monkey told us that we must all die. We won't even live as long as trees."

Now this story tells two things. It tells why human beings die. And it tells that bad news, like gossip, travels faster than good.

INSIGHTS

This myth is from the Zulu people, whose homeland is in southern Africa. At one time, the Zulu nation was a warrior kingdom. In the 18th century, all young unmarried men had to serve in the Zulu army. A man couldn't even get married without the king's permission.

Today many of the two and a half million Zulus mine gold and diamonds.

As in "Why Folks Must Die," many African myths about death involve a problem with a message. Sometimes there are two different messengers. Sometimes there is one mixed-up message.

For example, some among the Nuer people say that the creator didn't know how long people would live. So he threw a piece of gourd into the water. If it floated, people would live forever. If it sank, people would have to die. The gourd floated!

God then sent a woman to share the good news with everyone else. The woman tried to show the people how God had made his decision. But she mistakenly threw a piece of a clay pot into the water. Of course, the heavy piece of pottery sank, so people had to die.

GODS AND MORTALS

The Poor-Minded Servant

How People Came to Be Different

The Man Who Argued with God

Most native African religions have one high god, with several lesser gods under him.

African mythology is full of people who don't understand the High God or who question his actions. Sometimes the people are punished for demanding too much of him. But other times the people are patiently taught the High God's point of view.

In either case, the people are given the opportunity to learn lessons that would help them live a better life.

THE POOR-MINDED SERVANT

VOCABULARY PREVIEW

Below is a list of words that appear in the story. Read the list and get to know the words before you read the story.

ancestors—ancient relatives; past family
invaluable—priceless; very valuable
favor—goodwill
mock—pretend; false
rebuking—scolding
timid—lacking courage

Main Characters

King of Kumasi—poor man's master
Nyambi—High God
Nyambi Ana—son of Nyambi
Poor man—servant of the King of Kumasi

THE

A poor man grew tired of being poor. So he complained to Nyambi, the Great God. Nyambi gave the man two chances to make his life better. But the man only proved that poor-minded people are poor for a reason.

OOR-MINDED
SERVANT

Adapted from an Ashanti legend

Now know the story of why certain folks who are poor will always stay that way.

There was once a poor man who farmed for the King of Kumasi.[1] He woke up poor, worked all day poor, and went to bed poor. His father and his father's father and his father's father's father were poor too.

Now there are many people who are poor. But this man would always complain about being poor. All his relatives before him had done the same thing.

---

umasi is the capital city of the Ashanti kingdom. It is located in Ghana.

"My life is wasted in the dust because of the God Nyambi,"[2] he would say. "Nyambi is the richest of the gods, yet he makes me suffer."

One day the man's words reached the ears of Nyambi. Concerned, Nyambi sent his son Nyambi Ana[3] down from the sky to bring the man back. Nyambi Ana did as he was asked and brought the man to his father's heavenly village. In this village lived **ancestors** of all the families on earth.

"I'm told," said Nyambi, "that you fuss about being poor. Since you are so unhappy, I'll let you change families. Pick out the family that you would rather be part of. See if that makes things better for you. But remember, it is not I who causes your suffering."

The man carefully studied all the families. There were so many! He could choose to be part of a very rich family. He could choose to be part of a family that was very poor. Or he could choose any other in-between stage of family life.

But the man was **timid** at heart and afraid of trying new things. So when he saw his own family, he immediately selected it.

Nyambi nodded. "As you know, your family has never enjoyed material wealth. There are no riches there now, and there never will be. Yet that is the family that you have chosen to return to."

Nyambi paused and studied the man. Then he said, "I will go even further for you. I will give you the chance to change your condition and your future. I shall give you a gift."

As the man watched with hungry eyes, Nyambi produced two sacks: one tiny and one huge. "One is for you," Nyambi said. "The other you must give to your master—the King of Kumasi. You must choose wisely. I will not tell which you should keep for yourself and which you should give to the king."

After begging his leave from Nyambi, the poor man took both sacks and returned to earth. But before he presented him-

---

[2] (nē yam´ bē)
[3] (nē yam´ bē a´ na)

self to the king, he hid the big sack in a field hog's burrow. He had to act quickly, for he didn't want to be seen. Even though he didn't look into the bags, he was sure that the large sack was full of gold or some other **invaluable** substance.

Then the poor man prepared himself to meet his master. He was very nervous. He was afraid the king would be angry with him for being away from the fields.

The man met with a surprise. Instead of **rebuking** him for his absence, the king asked about his trip. "So you have been to visit Nyambi," the king said with **mock** interest. "Tell me, does the Supreme Ruler have a message for me?"

"The God Nyambi gives you this gift," the man said.

The king smiled. "How kind it was of Nyambi to think of me." He figured the sack was actually from the man to get back into his **favor.**

But when the king opened the little sack, he let out a cry of wonder. Inside he found gold dust worth a fortune. At once he realized that the gift could not have been from his servant.

Horrified, the poor man rushed away to the field hog's hole. With shaking hands, he reached for the big sack. But when he opened it, he found only stones.

Then the voice of Nyambi spoke to him. "To be poor is not a crime. To be poor-minded is. The child of poor-minded parents never becomes rich. If he gains some wealth, it slips through his fingers. Poor-minded you are, and poor you will always be."

INSIGHTS

The word "Ashanti" can describe a people, a language, or a kingdom. The great kingdom the Ashanti people once ruled is now the country of Ghana in western Africa.

In Ashanti tradition, stools are more than just seats—they're also homes for the souls of the dead.

The Ashanti believe that when a person dies, the soul of the dead person continues to live in that person's personal stool. Families often have a special "stool house" where they keep the stools of their ancestors.

The Ashanti also have a stool for their entire nation. The story of this stool is told in a legend.

In the 18th century, a neighboring kingdom tried to conquer the Ashanti. A medicine man named Anochi prayed to the High God for help. In answer, a Golden Stool came down from the sky. Anochi told the people that the stool held the soul of the nation. United by the Golden Stool, the Ashanti overthrew their enemy.

The Golden Stool is still kept in the royal palace at Kumasi. Some believe that if the stool is ever stolen, great harm will come to the Ashanti.

The Ashanti are also famous for their "talking drums." In many African languages, the meaning of a word often depends on its pitch. So drums can "talk" by imitating the pitches of words.

A drum message can be heard up to seven miles away. If the message is important, those who hear it will send it on to the next village. Eventually the message gets to the right person because everyone has a special drum name.

HOW PEOPLE CAME TO BE DIFFERENT

VOCABULARY PREVIEW

Below is a list of words that appear in the story. Read the list and get to know the words before you read the story.

discord—argument; conflict
distracted—confused; bothered
obsessed—caught up in; excited
predict—tell the future; forecast
recounted—repeated
unique—different; one of a kind
vices—moral weaknesses; bad habits

Main Characters

Chameleon—messenger for Olorun
Great Thinker—man full of ideas
Obatala—god who created humans
Olorun—High God

*The first people had everything
they needed. But they weren't
satisfied and asked for more.
These foolish people forgot how
dangerous it can be to get exactly
what you ask for.*

How People Came to Be
DiFFerenT

Inspired by a Yoruba tale

In the Yoruba city of Ife[1] the
High God Olorun[2] kept all the
people happy. No one had less
than another. No one had
more than another. Everyone
had the same color of hair,
eyes, and skin. Life was good.

Oh, there were a few peo-
ple who were shaped differ-
ently, but no one really
noticed. This happened
because Obatala[3] was drunk
with palm wine when he created the first people. You see,

---

[1] (ē´fay) Ife is a city in western Nigeria.
[2] (ōl´ ōr un) Olorun is the Supreme God of the Yoruba people.
[3] (ōb a tal´ a) Obatala is the creator of humans. (See "Obatala Creates the World,"
pp. 11-17.)

he dropped a few on the ground by mistake. The person who fell on his head was called the Great Thinker.

This one thought long, long, long thoughts and made long, long, long speeches. People usually would nod politely at him and go on about their business.

One day the Great Thinker finished a particularly long thought. Then he began an equally long speech. "Why must we all be the same color?" he asked. "Why is it that no one has more or less than another? Isn't this way of life boring to you?"

People had begun to gather around, so the thinker spoke on. "Olorun answers each of our needs the same way. Wouldn't you like to be **unique?** Wouldn't you like to have things no one else has?"

The thinker became **obsessed** with this thought. The more people listened, the more he carried on and on about it. Finally others began to agree with him.

"It would be nice to have a house that doesn't look the same as everybody else's," said one man. "Often I've gone into my neighbor's home by mistake."

"Obatala gives every family a firstborn at the same time," said a woman. "When we hold our naming ceremonies, everybody else does too. Then we give our children the same name. It would be better to hold individual ceremonies and give our children different names."

That's how it began. More and more people began to grumble and complain about the sameness of everything. They began to argue with each other too. When people argued, the noise attracted quite a crowd. No one had ever argued in Ife before. Soon after the arguments started, gossip appeared among the people. Soon came greed and other **vices.**

The **discord** became so loud that it reached Olorun's ears. Of course, being the Supreme Ruler, he hesitated to visit Ife himself. Instead, he sent his special messenger, Chameleon, to find out what the problem was.

However, Chameleon was a rather slow messenger. You see, he was easily **distracted.** With each eye, separately, he looked at every single thing along his path. With each ear, separately, he listened to every single noise. Needless to say, when he reached Ife, he got both eyes and both ears full.

"Give me this! Give me that! More cloth! More palm nuts! More hoes! More gold, silver, drums, goats, children, wives, seeds, houses, jewelry! More, more, more—but just for me!"

The people of Ife wanted different colors of hair and different shades of skin. Some thought lighter skin was prettier. Others thought darker skin was better. People even asked for different colors of rain to fall upon their crops.

"Great Olorun, it's a mess," Chameleon said when he returned. He **recounted** for Olorun every single desire that every single person of Ife had expressed. Three days later, he finished listing the requests of the people of Ife.

"I will grant their every wish right now," Olorun said. "But I **predict** that they will not be happy anymore. In a year's time, go back down and see how they're doing."

A year later Chameleon returned to Ife. He found the people in an uproar. Their desires had all been met, but this had only made things worse.

Chameleon first stopped before a small group of men and women. "The Great Olorun sends this message," he began. "Your wishes have been granted. But—"

"And it's all your fault!" a woman interrupted angrily. "You should have told Olorun to give me what I wanted *after* my neighbor received her wishes. I asked for two goats, five pieces of gold, and red hair. My neighbor saw my gifts and asked for *three* goats, *ten* pieces of gold, and *blonde* hair. And now she has more. She brags! Such nerve!"

The women and men began to argue among themselves. They even threw rocks at each other. Poor Chameleon crawled into a grove of palm trees and watched from there. He sent up a prayer for help to Olorun.

"Enough is enough," said Olorun when he heard Chameleon's prayer. "The people want to be different! We'll give them just what they want!"

In the twinkle of an eye, Olorun gave the arguing people different languages. From that day forward, the people could not understand one another. Then Olorun scattered the people to all corners of the land.

Since that time, people have realized their mistake. Every so often, people try to understand each other and overcome their differences. But after a short time, greed, gossip, and misunderstandings rise up again. So it has been ever since the Great Thinker thought his foolish thoughts.

INSIGHTS

The chameleon is an important animal in African mythology. Stories about this creature are found all over the continent.

In many myths, the chameleon delivers the High God's messages to humans. However, in Zaire the chameleon itself is considered a god. And in the Congo, the Pygmies pray to the chameleon when they need rain.

Africans respect the chameleon because it moves cautiously and silently. Thus it symbolizes wisdom. Some peoples even claim to be descended from the wise chameleon.

"How People Came to Be Different" briefly mentions Yoruba naming ceremonies. For some Yoruba parents, choosing a baby's name is not a task to be taken lightly. The fact that the names chosen are often similar to those of the gods proves how important naming is.

The day the naming ceremony is held depends on the sex of the child. If the baby is a girl, she is named on the seventh day after birth. If the baby is a boy, he is named on the ninth day after birth. Because twins are special to the Yoruba, the eighth day after birth is set aside just for their naming.

The Yoruba are not the only African people to have a story about people wanting too much. The Basotho of southern Africa tell about a young prince who demanded that the King give him the moon. His foolish father gave in to the prince's demand and promised to get it for him. The King had a great tower built that reached all the way to the sky. But the man who tried to bring down the moon poked a hole in it, causing a great explosion. The King, the prince, and all the people were killed.

The moon still shines in the heavens, but the greedy people and their entire country were destroyed.

THE MAN WHO ARGUED WITH GOD

VOCABULARY PREVIEW

Below is a list of words that appear in the story. Read the list and get to know the words before you read the story.

astonishment—great surprise; amazement
brooded—sulked; grieved
mourning—grief; sadness caused by death of a loved one
pleas—requests; appeals
radiated—shone in all directions
serenity—calm; peace of mind
vanity—self-love

Main Characters

Chagga man
Great One—High God
Wife of Chagga man

*"All that God does is good,"
says an African proverb. But a
father whose children died
didn't believe it. The grieving
man vowed to kill God. Here is
what happened when he met
God face-to-face.*

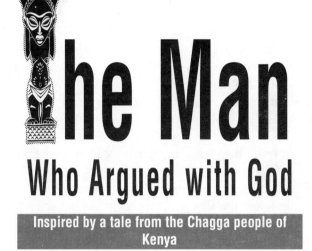

The Man
Who Argued with God

Inspired by a tale from the Chagga people of
Kenya

In the Chagga[1] kingdom there lived a man and a
woman who had ten fine children—five sons and
five daughters. But these children all died and
went to heaven to be with God. They left their
father and mother behind.

The man became very angry with God for
having taken his children. He endlessly **brooded**
over this tragic event. His wife was in **mourning**
too. But she accepted the will of God. She begged
her husband to keep the faith, for God knew best.

---

[1] The homeland of the Chagga people is on the border between Kenya and
Tanzania.

But the man cursed God to his friends and enemies alike. His friends offered prayers. His enemies offered revenge.

"Kill God," his enemies said. "Go to the spearmaker for ten sharp spears. Use them to kill the one who killed your children—especially your sons."

The foolish man did as his enemies said. Ignoring the **pleas** of his wife, he set out to find the place where God lived. He carried ten sharp spears to kill God with—one spear for each dead child.

The man walked and he walked through many lands. In each village he asked where God lived. Nobody knew.

Finally he stopped an old man. "Where does God live?" he asked. "I seek revenge from him for taking my children."

"Be blessed it was God and not the devil who took your children," the old man replied. "Be blessed that you even had sons and daughters. All things work for good when God is involved. Let your anger pass and praise God for his wisdom. You will be rewarded for your faith."

"You're no help," the angry man said and continued his search for God.

Finally the man came to an ocean. There he found crowds of people lining the shores. The people buzzed and hummed with excitement. As the man watched, a griot[2] passed by and strode out upon the beach. "Make way for the King of all Men!" the griot shouted.

Then in the center of the crowd, a tall Black man appeared. Around him a golden light **radiated**.

The angry man quickly hid in a grove of palm trees.

Cries rose and fell like the waves of the sea. "All praise to the Great One!" the people shouted. The Black man smiled upon the crowd. Then, to the **astonishment** of the man, the Great One walked straight to the palm trees where he had hidden. The Great One spread wide his arms.

"Welcome, my son. You're the man who holds such sorrow and anger against me."

The man said nothing.

---

[2] (grē´ ō) A griot is a historian and storyteller of western Africa who performs community histories.

"Yes, your children are now with me," the Great One said. "If you still wish to get revenge by spearing me, I am here. But before you do, please see your sons and daughters."

The Great One motioned to ten young people standing in the crowd. They came forward and embraced their father. The man then saw that his children were the same and yet not the same.

On earth their faces had held expressions of pride, **vanity,** greed, anger, ignorance, and other traits of human weakness. But now the father saw that their faces shone with **serenity** and happiness.

The words of the old man came back to the Chagga man. He realized that the Great One's will was best. He dropped his spears to the ground. "My children belong to you," the man said. "My faith was weak. Please forgive me."

"That you seek forgiveness shows your faith is still strong," the Great One said. "Return to your wife and remember your blessings and your faith. With faith comes riches."

The man returned home to his loyal wife and vowed to renew his faith. He planted his crops and tended them without complaint. He sang the praises of God to all who would listen. He learned not to listen to his enemies.

After a year his wife announced that she was with child, and they rejoiced when she gave birth to a son. In time more sons and daughters were born to them. Because of their faith, the Chagga man and his wife grew rich beyond their imaginations.

INSIGHTS

The homeland of the Chagga people is in Kenya, a country on the east coast of Africa. Most of the Chagga live in the highlands, where they farm the rich soil.

These people have a unique farming custom. What they grow depends on whether they are male or female.

For instance, only the women grow beans, sweet potatoes, and yams. And only men grow bananas. Both men and women grow corn.

The Chagga speak one of the many Bantu languages. The first Bantu speakers lived in the Congo River basin in west central Africa. From there, they moved to eastern and southern Africa.

This migration began over 2,000 years ago, during the Iron Age. At first, the Bantu moved east, to the Great Lakes region. But that area became crowded, so some tribes moved south. By 300 A.D., the Bantu had spread to what is now South Africa. Today, more than two-thirds of all Africans are descended from these Bantu migrants.

As they traveled, the Bantu taught other people to raise cattle and use iron farm tools. They also spread their language. Today over 500 variations of the Bantu language are spoken in central and southern Africa.

Most Bantu languages are genderless. That is, they do not have words like "he" and "she." Only a person's name indicates whether that person is male or female.

Bantu homesteads generally don't have a large family house. Instead, many separate huts serve specific functions. One hut is for unmarried boys; another is for single girls. Then there is a separate hut for each wife and her children. Another hut serves as a kitchen and still another as a food storage hut.

TRICKSTERS

Tortoise Cracks His Shell

Brother Spider Gets Stuck

Hare Causes Big Trouble

Tricksters are found in myths all over the world. They are often small animals who cause big trouble.

Africans tell stories about several different tricksters. Three of the most popular tricksters are Tortoise, Spider, and Hare. Each of these tricksters is something like the animal he's named after. But each has some human and supernatural qualities too. In fact, some groups honor the trickster as a god.

Trickster myths are often humorous. Even when tricksters get into trouble, there's no cause to worry. They just bounce back and start more trickery.

TORTOISE CRACKS HIS SHELL

VOCABULARY PREVIEW

Below is a list of words that appear in the story. Read the list and get to know the words before you read the story.

buff—polish
compliment—praise
concern—business
discarded—thrown away
glossy—bright and shiny
sported—showed off
valet—servant

Main Characters

Buzzard—friend of Monkey and Tortoise
Monkey—Tortoise's friend and servant
Tortoise—trickster

Tortoise usually got what he wanted. But sometimes his lack of self-control landed him in trouble. In this story, Tortoise's pride causes his fall.

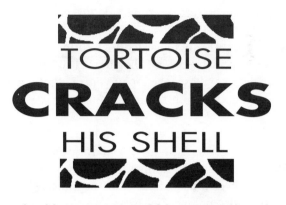

TORTOISE CRACKS HIS SHELL

Inspired by numerous African tortoise tales

Don't let Tortoise's version of how his shell was broken stir your sympathy. It's his own fault—and no one else's—that his shell is cracked. Monkey, who was Tortoise's personal **valet,** knows the whole story.

Tortoise once **sported** a brilliant yellow undershell. It was as smooth and shiny as an elephant's tusk. Everybody said Tortoise's shell was the most beautiful thing around.

Well, his friends—Monkey and Buzzard—*told* Tortoise everybody said so. Tortoise got quite vain over such praise—particularly the praise of Monkey. So he hired Monkey to wax his undershell with palm oil. Monkey would **buff** the shell with Buzzard's **discarded** feathers. Then he would polish Tortoise's toenails with red berry juice.

Monkey kept Tortoise right side up too. (He did that for free.)

One day Buzzard suggested that Tortoise lie on his back and have a special weekend showing. "The way you sit now, the animals can only see the top of your shell. If you turn over, even the goats high on the mountains will see your undershell."

Tortoise thought that was a great idea.

"I'm not so sure," Monkey told Tortoise when they were alone. "I saw Buzzard lick his lips when he made that suggestion. All he ever thinks about is his next meal. If you turned over, you'd dry up and die. Next thing you know, you'd be breakfast for Old Baldbrain. You stick with me and you won't go wrong."

One day Monkey was waxing, buffing, polishing, and praising Tortoise. "Your shell is almost as bright as the sun himself," Monkey told him.

This, indeed, was the highest **compliment** Tortoise had ever heard. "Pour a little more oil on me, right in the middle where my wide spots are."

"And, Tortoise, the sun couldn't hold a candle to you. You're so bright you could make crops grow—I bet you could even dry up lakes."

"Really?" Tortoise blushed and began to think great thoughts. "I could make grass grow and make water disappear? That's big time!"

Monkey began to sing. He used up half a bottle of oil and fifteen buzzard feathers listening to himself.

You could hang up there in the sky all day.
Knock that old sun out of the way.
Bright all day and bright all night.
Either way you go, you'd be dynamite!

All afternoon Tortoise thought about himself and the sun. He decided that Monkey was right. He looked around until he saw Buzzard in a tree not far away.

"Buzzard, do you think my shell is shiny?" Tortoise asked.

"Just thinking how **glossy** it is myself," said Buzzard. Actually Buzzard had been listening to his own stomach growl.

"Is it really as bright as the sun?"

"Just as bright, if not brighter."

Tortoise got so excited he began to pant. "So bright it could grow crops and dry up lakes?" he cried. "That's what Monkey told me. He said I should hang up in the sky all day and knock the old sun out of the way."

"Well, why not?" said Buzzard, who never believed a word Monkey said.

"Then that settles it. Buzzard, will you take me up into the sky? I want to start raising crops and drying up lakes."

"Be happy to," said Buzzard. He didn't ask how Tortoise was planning to *stay* in the sky. That wasn't his **concern.**

Tortoise clumsily pulled himself onto Buzzard's back. Buzzard lifted his wings and carried Tortoise into the air. Soon the two animals were soaring high over the land.

Tortoise was excited. He imagined himself making the corn grow and causing the yams to sprout. He pictured the animals' surprise when he rose in the east the next morning.

Tortoise couldn't wait any longer. He waved his paw in the air. "This spot looks good. Just let me off right here."

"Okay, here you go," Buzzard said as he shook Tortoise off his back.

However, Tortoise didn't hang in the sky. He fell straight to the ground and bounced three times.

When Tortoise regained consciousness, he was thankful to see that he was still in one piece. But his shell wasn't. Pieces were scattered all over the ground. Monkey was picking them up and putting them in a basket.

"You and Old Baldbrain sure get some great ideas," Monkey said with disgust.

Tortoise hurt too much to answer. For a small fee, Monkey patched Tortoise's shell back together. He didn't do a very good job, though.

Now whenever anyone comes near, Tortoise pulls his head inside his shell. He's ashamed of his cracked shell and his vanity that led to his fall.

INSIGHTS

Africans have many stories about Tortoise. They admire his ability to survive. There is a Swahili song about his tough shell: "I move house and yet I never move house. I'm at home wherever I travel."

Tortoise is protected by his wits as well as his shell. For example, in one myth Tortoise was caught by a lion. Tortoise reminded Lion that his shell was too tough to chew. But if Lion just put him in the river, his shell would soften. The hungry lion threw Tortoise into the water, and the trickster escaped.

In another tale Tortoise used his quick wits to win a race with Hare. Tortoise asked members of his family to line up all along the racetrack. Hare ran as fast as he could, but a tortoise always appeared ahead of him.

The Yoruba call the Tortoise *Ijapa*. They have many proverbs about this trickster. Some of these wise sayings are about ways people should be like Ijapa. For example, "It is a cautious person like a tortoise who can see a tortoise in the bush." This means that if you stay alert, you won't be tricked.

However, other proverbs show the Tortoise acting in ways people should never behave. For example, Ijapa once went to a feast with his son hidden in his pocket. Every time the Tortoise put a bite of food in his mouth, he put another in his pocket. However, his trick was discovered. Ever since, saying that someone gives "one morsel to the mouth, one to the pocket" means that person is dishonest.

BROTHER SPIDER GETS STUCK

VOCABULARY PREVIEW

Below is a list of words that appear in the story. Read the list and get to know the words before you read the story.

ambled—strolled; walked slowly
arrogance—disregard; disrespect
desperation—despair; sorrow
hearty—warm; cheerful
hobbled—limped; walked lamely
reputation—a person's status or character as seen by others
reserve—supply; stock

Main Characters

Brother Spider—trickster; husband of Sister Spider
Sister Spider—wife of Brother Spider

Africans say, "The wisdom of the spider is greater than that of all the world put together." But one time Spider was too clever for his own good. In this story, the trickster is finally tricked.

Brother Spider Gets Stuck

Inspired by a Hausa tale

Sister Spider and her husband Brother Spider were ordinary spiders of the garden variety. Of course, garden spiders are famous for being excellent farmers. But Brother Spider preferred to think instead of farm. No, he wasn't lazy. One cannot be lazy and also think, because thinking takes work.

The rest of the villagers were garden spiders too. They spent all their time farming and talking about farming. They also gossiped about Sister Spider's husband.

Don't get me wrong. They appreciated thinking and thinkers. But they didn't appreciate Brother Spider's way of thinking, which usually involved a good deal of palm wine and long naps. His kind of thinking didn't put food on the table.

Come each spring, everybody else tilled the soil, planted seeds, and weeded their crops. Sister Spider, who had arthritis[1] in all her legs, did what she could. Come each fall, everybody else harvested crops. Sister Spider, who also had a bad back, harvested the few crops she had. Come each winter, everybody else had food. But Sister Spider usually had to beg food from her daughter-in-law.

Sister Spider had also tried weaving cloth and exchanging it for food in the market. But now her arthritis kept her from such work.

This particular spring, Sister Spider was mighty worried. She didn't know how she could get the crop planted.

Sister Spider turned to her husband. She found him lying on a grass mat, eating beans. As usual, he was thinking.

"Can you help me with the planting today?" she asked.

"Tomorrow for sure," Brother Spider replied. "Do we have seeds?"

Sister Spider frowned. "I thought we had seeds from our daughter-in-law's old crop."

Brother Spider stopped chewing. "Oh no, they shriveled up long ago. Without seeds, we can't plant our crops. Let me think about that."

Sister Spider was old, but she wasn't a fool. You don't get to be old being a fool. She knew that the very beans Brother Spider was eating were the last of their tiny **reserve** of seeds.

Sister Spider sighed. Once again, she went on over to her daughter-in-law's home and begged eight handfuls of seeds from her.

---

[1] Arthritis causes the joints of the body to swell and become painful.

The next morning Sister Spider cornered her husband. "We now have seeds," she said. "Can you help prepare the ground?"

"I would gladly have turned over the ground long ago," Brother Spider said. "But you didn't get the hoe sharpened, remember? Let me think about how we can get that done."

What Sister Spider remembered was that Brother Spider had lost the hoe last fall. So she again went to her daughter-in-law's home and borrowed an old rusty hoe. Then she patiently scraped the blade against a rock until it was sharp.

The next morning Sister Spider gave her husband the hoe and the seeds. With a shrug of his shoulders, Brother Spider went off to the fields. Every day that summer he went to the fields. Meanwhile, Sister Spider repaired her loom and tried her hand at weaving cloth again.

When harvest time arrived, Sister Spider saw everybody else bring home food. But Brother Spider brought home no food.

Curious and hungry, Sister Spider decided to visit Brother Spider in the field. She found him on his grass mat. His legs were crossed one upon the other, upon the other, upon the other. And upon the other and the other and the other and the other. He was eating dried yams and drinking palm wine. Sister Spider frowned when she saw him get up and hide his refreshments in a hole and cover it over.

"That lazy Brother Spider! I should have known!" said Sister Spider as she **hobbled** back home. She was as mad as her cousin the hornet. "I'll fix him," she said to herself.

Back home, she cut out the figure of a female spider from a strip of bark. Then she carefully smeared the figure with sticky fruit gum. With a glint in her eye, she took the figure back to the field. This time, she found Brother Spider asleep on the ground.

Quietly she set the figure on top of the covered hole where Brother Spider had put his palm wine. Then she hid.

Presently Brother Spider woke up. "I must have a quick snack before I go home to Ol' Grumble Lips," he said aloud.

Grumble Lips! Sister Spider almost came out from her

hiding spot.

Just then Brother Spider saw the figure at his hiding place. "Ho! And who are you? A thief! Be gone!" he roared.

Brother Spider looked again. "Oh, a lady!" he murmured.

Pulling up his stomach, Brother Spider **ambled** over to the figure. In a **hearty** voice, he bid her hello.

The figure, of course, said nothing. Angered by her **arrogance,** Brother Spider lifted one of his arms. "Playing hard to get, Miss Uppity? Speak up, or else I'll bounce you a couple on both sides of your face!"

The creature stayed quiet.

"Warned you! Here I go!"

Spider smacked the creature—Blam! Blam!—on the left side of its head. Then Spider smacked it—Blip! Blip!—on the right side. Brother Spider tried to pull back, but to his horror, he found two of his arms stuck fast to the sticky girl's head.

"Let go! I'm a married man!" Brother Spider shouted. "Telling you, woman, to cut me loose, or I'll kick you in the knees! No? Well then, take this and this and this and this!"

Brother Spider kicked the spider girl—Bop! Bop!—in her left knees and then—Bap! Bap!—in her right. Of course, his legs stuck fast.

Sister Spider, watching from behind a tree, couldn't help chuckling at the sight. Then she began to laugh. She laughed so hard she fell back on the ground. She threw all her arms over her mouth to hold in the sound. Then she sat up and peeped out again.

"Humph! Let me go, I said!" Brother Spider shouted. "My wife'll be coming along any minute. I'll tell her you ate our crops. You'll be in deep trouble when she gets here!"

Brother Spider jerked and pulled, but he couldn't get loose. Finally, in **desperation,** he hit the fruit gum girl with his head. Of course, all of Brother Spider was stuck to the creature now.

Sister Spider laughed so hard she had to hang on to the tree. Then she sat down and peeped out again.

"Oh, please let me go," Brother Spider begged the fruit gum girl. "I'll never say a word about this to anybody. Now just let me loose before the other folks leave their fields and see us like this. You know, it won't be good for your **reputation.** And I'll never live it down that I got beat up by some ol' sticky fruit gum girl."

Of course, that didn't work. Presently Brother Spider began to hear voices in the distance. The other folks were beginning to leave their fields.

Brother Spider began to cry. "Oh please, Miss Sticky Lady, let me loose. I let Sister Spider think I've been raising crops out here, but I haven't planted a thing. I admit that I haven't done my duty. But if you let me go, I'll change my ways!"

At these pitiful words, Sister Spider felt sorry for her husband. She sent up a prayer to the rain god. She asked him to wash Brother Spider loose from the sticky woman. Then she started back home. Just as she was about to enter the house, it began to rain.

Before long, Brother Spider came home. He sheepishly slipped in, sopping wet and smelling like fruit.

"You know, I've been thinking. I think I'll give up farming. And while I'm at it, I may as well give up palm wine too. I'd much rather help you right here at home. I think I'll try something new."

Brother Spider pulled Sister Spider's old loom into their house and set it in the corner. He figured out how to weave in record time. He got so good at it, all the other spiders learned how to weave too. They've been doing it ever since, especially in the corners of people's homes.

INSIGHTS

The African spider trickster is often called *Anansi*. In most tales about Anansi, he manages to outsmart his rivals. Indeed, Spider is so cunning that he sometimes acts as the High God's chief official.

But on occasion, Spider's tricks backfire. That's when he becomes the object of his own jokes. However, don't let that fool you. Anansi is still a trickster. One African proverb warns, "Woe to him who would put his trust in Anansi—a sly, selfish, and greedy fellow."

Tales about Spider are common throughout Africa. The story presented here is told among the Hausa people near Nigeria.

The Hausa were originally organized in seven independent city-states. In the 1500s, Muslim traders from northern Africa began winning converts to Islam. Today the majority of the estimated nine million Hausa are Muslims.

Stories about Spider are also told in America. Here Anansi is often called Nansi or Annancy.

The most popular story that parallels "Brother Spider Gets Stuck" is "The Tar Baby." It is one of the most popular stories in African-American folklore.

HARE CAUSES BIG TROUBLE

VOCABULARY PREVIEW

Below is a list of words that appear in the story. Read the list and get to know the words before you read the story.

complement—go together; balance
distinguished—dignified; elegant
nuisance—bother; pest
privately—secretly; individually
snubbed—insulted; put off
statuesque—huge; great; impressive

Main Characters

Hare—trickster
Hippo—friend of Rhino
Rhino—friend of Hippo

Hippo and Rhino were the best of friends. But to these two colossal animals, the Hare was just a small nuisance. With rumors and gossip, Hare found a way to get noticed.

Hare Causes Big Trouble

INSPIRED BY A SWAHILI TALE

It is said that Hippo and Rhino were once best friends. They thought of each other as **statuesque** in size and **distinguished** in looks. They shared the same tick bird[1] to rid them of bugs. They drank from the same watering hole. They even slept in each other's wallows.[2]

Now Hare was jealous of the larger animals' friendship. Hare talked about the two animals behind their backs. He said they were fat, greedy, loud, and ugly.

But Hare was all smiles to their faces. "Oh, you two have so much in common," he would say. "You **complement** each other."

While Hare made fun of the two large animals, he secretly wished that he could share their

---

[1] A tick bird eats insects that live on large animals.
[2] Wallows are mud holes that animals roll around in.

friendship. But every time he tried to make friends, he made a **nuisance** of himself. He danced on their heads when they lay in their wallows. He splashed in their drinking hole and muddied up the water.

All of this got their attention, but not their friendship.

One day Rhino and Hippo grew tired of Hare's silly behavior.

"Hippo, do you feel a flea?" asked Rhino when Hare hopped on Hippo's back.

"Either a flea or a fly," said Hippo as he rolled over on his back. The surprised Hare was nearly smashed by the large Hippo.

Well, Hare didn't take kindly to being called names. For days, he was angry at the way the two animals **snubbed** him. Finally Hare decided he must stand up for his honor. "If I can't enjoy the friendship of Hippo and Rhino," Hare said to himself, "then neither shall they!" He immediately got to work on a plan.

First he made a long rope from thick vines growing in the forest. Then he went to Rhino at the water hole.

"Hippo told me he's ten times stronger than you," Hare said slyly.

"That may be," Rhino laughed.

"He said you were ugly too," Hare went on.

Rhino suddenly remembered something. Hippo *had* said words to that effect many years ago—before they had become such good friends. It had made Rhino mad then, and it began to make him mad all over again.

"Tell me what else that ugly thing said," Rhino demanded.

"I don't know what Hippo had in mind," Hare continued innocently, "but he sent me to you with this rope. He said something about pulling you out of your sorry mud hole."

"Sorry mud hole, huh?" said Rhino, his voice rising. "You can tell him for me that I would be doing him a favor if I pulled him from that pig sty he lives in. Tie your rope to my back leg. Tell Hippo to prepare to find another home."

Hare took the other end of the rope and went in search of the other large animal. He found Hippo lying in his favorite wallow.

"Hippo," whispered Hare, "Rhino has been talking behind your back. He says you're weak and that your wallow smells like a pig sty."

"How's that?" said Hippo, who was a bit deaf.

Hare repeated his words. "He said he was tired of visiting your lousy mud hole. He says you're fat too." Hare held up the rope. "He challenges you to a tug of war."

Hippo thought this was strange talk to come from his friend of many years. But he remembered something mean Rhino had once said about him—something about how fat he was.

Hippo felt pride rise up inside his huge chest. "Tie that rope!" he roared.

Hare quickly tied the rope around Hippo's back left leg. "I'll tell you when to pull," Hare said. "By the way, Rhino also said you were ugly."

Hippo became enraged. He *knew* that he was much handsomer than Rhino ever could be. He charged off on his thick, short legs, pulling the rope tight. Rhino, feeling the tug, thundered away in the opposite direction.

Hare watched from a small hill. He laughed to see the two friends fighting against each other.

Hippo pulled and strained. "Say I'm fat?" he roared. "I'll show you!"

Rhino dug his feet into the ground and pulled hard too. "Think I'm ugly, do you? I'll show you!"

The rope, being only made of vines, popped. With a tremendous roar, both Hippo and Rhino fell over on their faces.

Hare gave out a shriek of laughter, lost his balance, and rolled right down the hill. He rolled first past Rhino, who got to his feet and gave chase. Then he rolled past Hippo, who prepared to follow. The two friends then came face to face.

"So I'm ugly, am I?" Rhino pawed the ground and shook his horn for battle.

"Well, you called me fat," shouted Hippo.

"I did no such thing," Rhino said back. "Hare told me

what you said."

Rhino stopped shouting. So did Hippo. They both turned to Hare, who ran off laughing.

Since that time, Hippo and Rhino have had only a polite friendship. They meet only at the watering hole—one on each side.

Jealousy—for that is Hare's real name—drinks there too. And he still whispers **privately** to each former friend about the other.

INSIGHTS

This story about the hare is from the Swahili culture. No one group can be called "Swahili." Swahili is a language spoken by many groups in eastern Africa. This language combines Bantu and Arabic.

In another version of this story, Hare tricks Elephant and Hippo into a tug of war. The larger animals get so angry at Hare for causing trouble that they won't let him eat grass or drink water. But Hare tricks them a second time. He claims to have a terrible illness that others can catch. So Elephant and Hippo run away before they get sick. Meanwhile, Hare stays behind and stuffs himself on grass and water.

The tug-of-war theme is so popular in Africa that there is even a dilemma story about it. This type of story ends with a question for the audience to answer.

In the dilemma story, Elephant and Hippo don't realize they've been tricked. They even admit that Hare is their equal. Then they let Hare sit with them in the highest places in the animal council. The question is: Are these animals really equal?

HOW AND WHY

How Lightning Came to Be

Why Mosses and Vines Grow on Trees

Why the Bat Sleeps Upside Down

How is lightning created? What causes people to fall in love? Why do bats sleep in caves?

Humans have asked questions like these since the beginning of time. And people have often looked to mythology for answers.

The three how and why myths in this section not only provide some interesting explanations. They also reveal the humor and wisdom of the African people who tell the stories.

HOW LIGHTNING CAME TO BE

VOCABULARY PREVIEW

Below is a list of words that appear in the story. Read the list and get to know the words before you read the story.

berserk—crazy; wild
distressed—alarmed; worried
empathy—understanding; concern
gnash—strike together; grind
roused—excited; stirred
suppress—hide; hold back

Main Characters

King—ruler of villagers and animals
Mother Sheep—mother of Ram
Ram—Mother Sheep's son

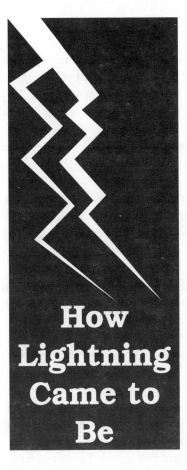

How Lightning Came to Be

Inspired by a Nigerian tale

The villagers were fed up with Ram's fussing and worrying. But should Ram be killed to end their misery? The king's solution explains why we sometimes shudder on a stormy night.

There was once a mother sheep whose son, Ram, loved her so much that he reacted to her every sound. If she sighed even softly, Ram became alarmed. If she gave a moan under her breath, he would **gnash** his teeth and toss his horns about. And if she groaned aloud, he became **distressed.**

This wouldn't have been so bad if Ram were an ordinary sheep. But he wasn't. His ironlike hooves created sparks whenever he walked on the rocky soil around his home. And when he was in distress over his mother, the sparks would fly! More than once, he had nearly burned their simple hut to the ground.

So it came to pass that whenever the villagers heard the voice of Mother Sheep, they would rush to fill buckets of water.

Once Mother Sheep forgot and "baa-ed" out loud from happiness. At once Ram rushed up and down among the homes in the village, spreading sparks left and right. His sparks set two fields of corn on fire. Another time he set two of the villagers' roofs aflame.

"My son," Mother Sheep would say. "Please don't alarm yourself over me. I'm just an old sheep. Nothing to get upset about."

"But, Mother, I can't help it," said the passionate young ram. "Anything that moves you in the least moves me even more."

One day Mother Sheep slipped and twisted her left front leg. Try as she might to **suppress** her pain, she couldn't help crying out sharply. An equally sharp cry rose up from the villagers. "Look out, here he comes! Water! Water!"

Ram went **berserk.** He galloped across fields and clearings. Sparks flew everywhere. Half the village burned to the ground.

The people angrily went to the king. "Do something before he fries us all," one old woman demanded. "We'd all be better off if Ram were killed," said another.

The king, however, was a kind-hearted fellow. He understood the son's **empathy** for his mother's feelings. He felt the same about his own beloved mother. When she became upset or moved by the slightest thing, he did too. Sometimes he became so **roused** by his mother's anger that he went to war.

So instead of having Ram killed, the king sent mother and son to live in the sky.

And they live there still. Sometimes you can hear Mother Sheep's voice in the thunder. And when lightning streaks across the sky, you can be sure that Ram is kicking up a fuss over his mother again.

INSIGHTS

This myth is from Nigeria, the homeland of the Yoruba people. Yoruba mythology tells of hundreds of gods—some major and others minor. Major gods, called the Orisha, rule huge regions such as the sky and earth. Minor gods rule over smaller areas such as villages.

What are the Orisha like? In many ways they resemble a family. Olorun is the father figure and rules over the sky. Olokun is the mother figure and rules over the earth.

The other gods act much like the children in a large family. They help each other, laugh at each other, and even plot against each other.

One of the most important Orisha is Shango, the god of thunder and lightning. Shango is an earth god. That is, he is a human being who became a god.

During his life, Shango was King of Oyo. At the end of his rule, Shango didn't die. Instead, he rose up to the sky along a golden chain and became the god of thunder and lightning. When the Yoruba hear thunder, they say *Kabiyesi!* This means, "Your Majesty, hail!"

Shango is also the god of fair play. He punishes those who lie, steal, and make evil magic. When he speaks, fire comes out of his mouth.

Shango's favorite wife is Oya, goddess of the River Niger. Oya is also known as the goddess of storms. When Shango rides the thunderstorms, Oya rides with him, blowing roofs off houses and uprooting trees.

WHY MOSSES AND VINES GROW ON TREES

VOCABULARY PREVIEW

Below is a list of words that appear in the story. Read the list and get to know the words before you read the story.

lush—thick; healthy
massing—gathering
mortally—resulting in death
petition—ask or request in a formal way
proposed—suggested
strikingly—uncommonly; unusually
valiantly—bravely

Main Characters

Amin—young man in love with Sayrah
Sayrah—beautiful young woman
Yengay—young man loved by Sayrah

Why do mosses and vines grow on trees? A romance from the Bambara people of western Africa gives one answer to this question.

Why Mosses and Vines Grow on Trees

Adapted from a Bambara tale

In a small village there lived a young Bambara man named Amin.[1] He deeply loved a young woman named Sayrah.[2]

However, Sayrah was devoted to a man named Yengay.[3] In fact, Sayrah and Yengay had been in love since they were very young. Everyone in the village knew about

[1] (a mēn´)
[2] (ser´ a)
[3] (yeng´ gā)

Sayrah and Yengay and expected them to marry.

But this didn't keep Amin from loving Sayrah. "My love is so great that I could even share her with Yengay," he declared. "But she must become my wife."

Amin asked his parents to **petition** Sayrah's father and mother for her hand. But they refused.

"Why must you be so blind?" asked Amin's mother. "This girl can feel nothing in her heart but love for Yengay. You would be unhappy with a woman like that for a wife."

Amin's parents tried to change his mind. First they brought him a young woman who was quite rich in farmland. Her fields were so grassy that cows left their pastures to graze in hers.

This young woman had admired Amin for some time. The whole village agreed that the young woman would make a good match for Amin.

But Amin said no. "I don't want land. I don't want cows. I want Sayrah."

His parents then brought him a young woman who was **strikingly** beautiful. When she walked, trees turned into firewood hoping to warm her feet. This young woman also had laid eyes on Amin—and she was interested. The villagers nodded their approval of this **proposed** match too.

Again Amin refused. "No woman is as beautiful in my eyes as Sayrah."

Well, this went on for some time. But Amin would have nothing to do with any women his parents found. Finally Amin's parents gave up. They talked with Sayrah's parents.

"Sayrah loves only Yengay," said the girl's parents. "But she may marry your son if she can bring Yengay to live with her. That is, if Yengay's parents approve of such an unusual arrangement."

And so it happened. Amin happily took Sayrah as his wife. But Sayrah brought Yengay with her.

Sayrah was obedient to Amin, but she remained faithful to Yengay. Before Sayrah served her new husband his dinner, she served Yengay. Before Amin's clothes could be washed, Sayrah washed Yengay's.

Amin soon realized that Sayrah loved Yengay more than she loved him. When he complained, she would gently remind him of their wedding agreement.

The village gossips took note of all of the goings-on in this strange household. "Amin is a fool," they said to each other. "Can't he see that Sayrah still loves Yengay?"

One day word came that the village was going to be attacked. In fact, the enemy was **massing** on the horizon. All unmarried men were to report to the king. Unmarried women would serve as cooks and nurses.

Since Yengay was still single, he immediately took up his spear and marched off to war.

With Yengay gone, Amin thought that he would have Sayrah to himself. But that night the enemy's armies began to march on the village. Things went badly for the village forces in the first attack. Everyone was asked to defend the village.

Sayrah immediately packed Amin's clothes. Then she packed hers. "I must go to Yengay," she told him. "He's on the front line."

"Can't we walk to the battle together?" Amin asked in despair.

"No. I want to walk alone," Sayrah said. "I'll meet you on the battlefield."

So Amin went alone with a heavy heart. When he arrived, he saw Yengay **valiantly** shooting arrow after arrow. Behind Yengay stood Sayrah.

Just then enemy arrows began to fall all around them. One hit Yengay and he fell to the ground. Another found its mark in Amin's chest. Sayrah screamed and rushed to the **mortally** wounded Amin.

"I love you, Amin," she whispered over and over. Her words reached the dying Amin's ears just in time. At last, in death, his love for Sayrah was returned. As Sayrah knelt beside him, another arrow found her heart.

It is said that where Sayrah died, a tree sprang up that gave no fruit. Where Yengay died, a strong, thick vine grew up the tree trunk. And where Amin died, **lush** green mosses spread across the ground. Eventually the moss covered both vine and tree.

You may not believe this. But the Old Ones say that this is why mosses and vines grow on trees.

INSIGHTS

This myth is from the Bambara people. The Bambara homeland is in western Africa, in what was once called Mali. In the 13th century, Mali was a large trading empire. Its rulers were famous for being just and fair.

Trade caravans brought the Islamic religion to Mali in the 1100s. Eventually, many people in both northern and western Africa became followers of Islam.

The Bambara are famous for their masks. Masks are used all over Africa in dances and religious rituals. But the Bambara have one mask that is found nowhere else.

This mask has two antelopes—a small one perched on top of a larger one. This unique headdress represents the *chi wara*—an important figure in Bambara tradition. The chi wara is a spirit who took the form of an antelope and taught the people to farm. Dancers wear these masks when they pray for a good harvest.

WHY THE BAT SLEEPS UPSIDE DOWN

VOCABULARY PREVIEW

Below is a list of words that appear in the story. Read the list and get to know the words before you read the story.

circumstances—conditions; events
dense—heavy; thick
dismay—fright; fear
ignorance—lack of knowledge; inexperience
laconic—brief; short
smirked—grinned; gave a stuck-up smile
stammered—stuttered

Main Characters

Bat—messenger for the High God
Chameleon—another messenger for the High God
High God—Supreme God
Monkey—another messenger for the High God

The poor bat was a nervous and uneasy creature. One time he became so embarrassed that he forgot the High God's orders. To this day, Bat is still trying to make up for his mistake.

Why the Bat Sleeps Upside Down

Inspired by a tale from the Kono people of Sierra Leone

In the beginning of time, Bat slept right side up. He leaned upright with his head tucked under his right wing, as chickens do.

Now Bat was a nervous sort. That's why he flipped and flapped and jerked when he flew.

One day a messenger from the High God appeared at Bat's door. The High God had an important task for the nervous animal. Bat was to present himself at the palace the next morning at eight o'clock sharp.

This was quite an honor for Bat. Usually the High God called upon Chameleon or Spider or Monkey to do his important work. But Bat was so nervous about serving the High God that he didn't sleep at all that night. And though Bat left for the palace two hours early, his wings trembled so much that he was half an hour late. Of course, being late made Bat even more nervous.

Finally God called Bat into His presence. "I have an important mission for you," God said in a stern voice. "This basket must be taken to the moon immediately."

God continued His orders as He slipped a little basket made of black and purple grasses around Bat's neck. "Go directly to the moon. Talk to no one. And under no **circumstances** should you look inside the basket."

With eager wings, the little Bat started on his mission.

Not far along, he saw Chameleon. Forgetting God's order, Bat called, "I'm a carrier for the High God."

Chameleon rolled one eye slowly up toward Bat. "What do you carry?" he asked in his **laconic** manner.

"This basket, for the moon." Bat lifted his chin proudly.

"What's in the basket?" Chameleon asked.

"Why, I don't know," Bat **stammered.** "God didn't say."

Chameleon dismissed Bat with an "umh humph" and slowly crawled on.

Bat sped on and soon flew over Monkey swinging in a tree.

"I'm a carrier for the High God," he sang.

"Congratulations," said Monkey. "And what do you carry?"

"This basket for the moon," Bat said.

The monkey asked him what was in the basket. When the Bat said he didn't know, Monkey **smirked.** "Some of us *carry* things and some of us just *haul* them."

Bat felt even more embarrassed at his **ignorance.** He flew down to the ground to a small clearing. Carefully he removed the basket from around his neck and set it on the ground. Slowly he pulled back the lid for a quick look.

Instantly a **dense,** dark shape swept out of the basket and flew up toward the moon. It covered everything with a deep velvet darkness.

With a cry of **dismay,** Bat darted after the darkness. But it was too late. Bat flew about for hours, trying to capture the darkness and return it to the basket.

But in time, the sun rose. Suddenly the darkness disappeared.

In fear of God's anger, Bat rushed home to his cave. Trying to hide from God, he hung himself upside down in a corner. He tucked both wings over his body and head and cried himself to sleep.

When Bat finally awoke, he saw that darkness had returned. Bat shot out into the dark night. He tried and tried to catch darkness to put it back in the basket.

"Please, darkness, return to this basket," he cried. "I must take you to the moon where you belong."

Of course, the darkness didn't reply. Nor did it climb into the basket.

To this day Bat chases darkness and sleeps upside down in caves. This is also how night came to be let loose into the world.

INSIGHTS

This story is from the Kono people of Sierra Leone in western Africa. Traditional Kono communities have an interesting educational practice. When young people reach the age of fifteen, they are initiated into secret societies—one for men and one for women.

The boys' initiation lasts from November to May. During this time, the boys stay in a special camp. They sleep on the ground and avoid people from the village. Older men teach the boys how to be adults. When the boys return to the village, they are considered men and they become members of the male secret society.

The Kono women have a similar but separate secret society with its own rituals.

Another explanation of why the bat hangs upside down in caves is told in a myth from the Congo. In this myth, the bat was a wealthy king. One day King Lightning paid Bat a visit. During the visit, Lightning spied a beautiful platter that belonged to Bat. Lightning asked King Bat if he could have the platter. But Bat refused, saying the platter was a symbol of his kingship.

Lightning became furious. He stormed back to the sky and destroyed all of King Bat's buildings and cattle. Because of Lightning's actions, King Bat vowed never to look toward the sky again. Instead, he hangs upside down in caves.

RIGHT AND WRONG

The Snake and the Princess

The Moon Prince

Point of View

While myths can be entertaining and fun to read, they can also teach moral lessons. Very often, the lessons are simple and straightforward. In general, humble and kind characters are rewarded. Selfish and greedy characters suffer in the end.

But sometimes a myth might present a character with a difficult life choice. For example, how should a prince handle his anger when an injustice is done to him? Or how should a young man act when asked to hide his true identity? The myths in this section deal with such difficult questions.

African storytellers often tell their listeners the moral or lesson of a story. But sometimes the tellers invite the audience to give their opinions. They might even stop the action of the story to ask the listeners what they think a character should do next.

Now it's your turn. What do you think?

THE SNAKE AND THE PRINCESS

VOCABULARY PREVIEW

Below is a list of words that appear in the story. Read the list and get to know the words before you read the story.

conniving—scheming; sneaky
controversy—argument
ebony—black
inherit—receive property from a relative
modesty—humbleness; self-control
pillaging—robbing; looting
spiteful—hateful; cruel
sullenly—gloomily
venom—poison

Main Characters

Ntombinde—princess
Queen Manyoka—mother of Snake Prince
Snake Prince—oldest son of Queen Manyoka

*He was a snake with the heart of a man. She was a princess
with the heart of a warrior. Only her courage could save
them both.*

The Snake and the Princess

Adapted from a tale from the Congo

In some ways, Ntombinde[1] was an ordinary princess.
She behaved just as you would expect a princess to
behave. She was compassionate and caring. And she
always thought of others before herself.

But in other ways, Ntombinde was a very extraor-
dinary princess. For example, she was very curious.
She often went exploring by herself, just to see how
other people lived.

---

[1] (tum bin´ dā)

But most of all, Ntombinde was very courageous. Once she fought off a band of thieves who were **pillaging** the countryside. Another time she challenged a river monster to a fight and triumphed.

Now the king was proud of his daughter. Yet he was embarrassed by her as well.

One day the king spoke to his wife about Ntombinde. "Where's her **modesty?**" he asked. "How will we ever find someone to marry her? She's just too outspoken. She must get that from you."

"I think that whoever becomes Ntombinde's lover will be a lucky man," the queen said with a playful smile. "For a *real* man, our daughter's courage and outspokenness will not be a threat. Who knows, Ntombinde may even save a man's life."

That spring Ntombinde was invited to a wedding many kingdoms away. As always, she traveled alone.

But along the way, night fell with Ntombinde far from her destination. As luck would have it, she came upon a small kingdom. She learned that it was ruled by Queen Manyoka[2]—widow of the late king. Ntombinde asked the queen for lodging at the royal palace.

Queen Manyoka graciously took her in and led her to a beautifully decorated room.

"Before I leave you, I must tell you the story of this room," the queen said. "Then you can decide if you wish to stay in it."

"I'm ready to listen," replied Ntombinde with enthusiasm. This sounded like an adventure and, as you know, Ntombinde loved adventure!

"Long ago, the king and I lived in happiness with our family," began the queen. "We had four children. Besides our eldest son, we had two younger sons and a daughter.

"Then **controversy** set in," continued the queen sadly. "The younger children thought it unfair that their oldest brother was to **inherit** the throne.

"Now our younger children were **spiteful** and lazy. On the

[2] (man yō´ ka)

other hand, our elder son was hardworking, intelligent, and caring. Little wonder he became our favorite child.

"We tried to keep the younger children happy. We even increased their inheritance. But as time went on, the three youngest became more and more jealous.

"Finally they paid an evil sorcerer[3] to get rid of their innocent brother. The sorcerer cast a spell that changed our beloved son into a snake."

The queen paused. With difficulty she finished her story. "The jealous action of our youngest children broke the king's heart. Finally he died of grief.

"The sad thing is, the young ones regretted their action. They were horrified by the sorcerer's power. Unfortunately they could do nothing to break the spell.

"We have since found out that only a maiden pure in heart can change my son back into a man."

"Have many women tried to save your son?" asked Ntombinde.

"Many have tried," Queen Manyoka replied. "But they only wanted our son's riches. He sensed their greed, and his snake heart hardened. He killed them all."

Queen Manyoka looked into Ntombinde's eyes. "Now do you still want to spend the night here?" she asked quietly.

"Yes," was Ntombinde's immediate reply. "I am curious to meet your son."

With that, the queen ordered a huge meal of meat and palm juice put on the table. Then she opened a window in the room. "Each night he returns to eat," she explained. "Perhaps you will be the one to bring a change of heart in my Snake Prince. Nothing else—not even the gods—can do it."

With these words, the queen turned and left the room.

Now common sense warned Ntombinde not to sleep near an open window. And she certainly didn't want to be surprised by a large snake. So she vowed to stay awake all night.

When daylight came, Ntombinde was still awake. The food was still there. But outside the window she found a patch

---

[3] A sorcerer is a magician.

of gold and black snakeskin.

"My son has been here," Manyoka said when she saw the skin. "And he didn't bother you. That's a good sign. Will you stay another night?"

The courageous Ntombinde agreed. Again Manyoka set out food and again Ntombinde stayed awake. In the morning the food remained uneaten. But this time servants found two patches of snakeskin outside.

"I think he's studying you," said Manyoka.

"I'm studying him too," said Ntombinde.

Manyoka asked Ntombinde to stay one more night. And now the younger sons and daughter begged her to stay too.

"You who made him suffer so now wish for his return?" Ntombinde asked with surprise. "Do you plan to give him yet more pain?"

"Oh no. All of this is our fault," admitted one brother.

"It was all so long ago," added the daughter. "We were selfish fools. Our tutors said we had the hardest heads in the whole kingdom."

"We were too busy listening to the gods of greed to learn anything," said the other brother. "And too lazy. We raced horses all day and danced all night. Now your courage is our only hope of bringing our brother back."

On this third night Ntombinde pretended to be asleep. Finally around midnight she heard a noise outside. Through half-closed eyes she saw a huge serpent glide in through the window. The Snake Prince coiled his golden-black body and lifted his head. Then he stared into Ntombinde's face.

The snake's face was that of a handsome man. Ntombinde had never seen such a sad face. Her heart melted as she fell in love with the Snake Prince.

But then the snake spoke. His face twisted into a mask of evil. "Why are you here?" he hissed harshly.

"Because you've already suffered more than most men ever will," Ntombinde replied. "And because your sadness touches my heart."

"You lie!" spat the snake. "You're just like all the rest. You hope to become my bride. And you want to be queen of this land so that you can get your hands on my riches."

"I don't need your riches," Ntombinde replied with fire in her eyes. "I'm already rich. I'm compassionate, curious, and courageous. And I'm not afraid to speak my mind."

"You lie. You're **conniving** and greedy." The snake towered over her. "I hate my brothers and sister for what they did to me. I hate everyone. First I'll kill you with my **venom.** Then I'll devour you."

The snake opened his mouth, showing his huge fangs. But Ntombinde stood her ground.

"Stop that!" Ntombinde said sternly. "In your heart you're still a man. But your heart has been poisoned by the hate of a snake. The ways of a snake cannot live in the heart of a man."

The snake was surprised by the young woman's outburst. He closed his mouth and stared at her in wonder.

But Ntombinde had just begun. "Devour me?" she laughed. "You do, and I'll give you a stomachache you won't forget. And if you call me a liar again, I'll stomp on your tail."

The Snake Prince pulled in his tail and backed away. "You're not big enough for a meal anyway," the snake said **sullenly.**

Still watching her, the snake slithered to the table and began to eat. Ntombinde thought she saw a smile dance briefly around the serpent's mouth.

Slowly Ntombinde approached the table. As if in a trance, the Snake Prince froze. Then without warning, the young princess gently kissed the prince on his snakeskin cheek.

The Snake Prince let out a deep sigh. The prince's human spirit broke through the snake's hateful hold on his heart. The snakeskin fell away.

Before Ntombinde stood a tall, handsome, **ebony**-skinned man wrapped in golden robes. The grateful prince immediately asked Ntombinde to marry him.

Ntombinde just smiled. "Let me see what my father has to say first."

INSIGHTS

The Snake and the Princess" comes from the Congo in central Africa. This part of Africa was isolated from the rest of the world for thousands of years. For this reason, the people of the Congo were unknown to the outside world until the 19th century.

The snake appears often in myths from the Congo. For example, the snake plays an important role in several creation stories from the region.

In one story, God called the first man and the snake together. Then he placed two baskets before them. Without saying what was in the baskets, God invited the man to choose one. The unlucky man chose the basket that contained death.

The snake was more fortunate. He got the basket that contained the secret of shedding his skin. By casting off his old skin for a new one, the snake learned how to live forever.

It's no wonder that snakes play important roles in myths from the Congo. A look at just one of the snakes of the region might explain why.

The African rock python is indeed impressive. This snake can grow up to 30 feet long and can reach a weight of 300 pounds. And this snake can be very dangerous—it has been known to swallow humans.

Despite this threat, many central Africans believe pythons help their crops grow. For this reason, farmers leave part of their fields unplowed. The farmers hope that a python will live in the unused area and make their land more fertile.

Snakes are important in other parts of Africa as well. According to the mythology of the Fon people of western Africa, a giant snake helped form the earth. Indeed, the snake still holds the world together. The serpent coils 3,500 times above the earth and 3,500 times below it. One Fon tradition says that if the snake ever moves, the world will fall apart.

THE MOON PRINCE

VOCABULARY PREVIEW

Below is a list of words that appear in the story. Read the list and get to know the words before you read the story.

apprentice—student; beginner
banished—sent away as punishment
coveted—much wanted; desired
decreed—ordered; commanded
flamboyant—showy; stylish
hearth—fireplace
heir—one who will become the next ruler
mockery—a joke

Main Characters

Ironsmith—foster father to Moon Prince
King Khoedi-Sefubeng—father of Moon Prince
Latifa—second favorite wife of the king
Moon Prince—son of the king and Morongoe
Morongoe—favorite wife of the king; mother of Moon Prince
Mouse—friend of Morongoe

Sometimes even small, humble creatures can make a big difference. In this story, you'll learn how Mouse helped the Moon Prince regain his rightful place.

THE MOON PRINCE

Inspired from a tale of the Sotho people

Mouse is the most humble of all creatures. She doesn't wear **flamboyant** feathers or flowing fur. Her voice is not pleasing to hear, and she cannot fly. Dressed simply in earth tones, Mouse industriously gathers seeds and straw for **hearth** and home.

Quiet and rarely seen, Mouse works hard and long during day and darkness. But not only for herself. She'll help anyone who needs her. They say she even helped the Moon Prince regain his rightful throne. This is how it happened.

Mouse lived in a cottage on the royal palace grounds of King Khoedi-Sefubeng.[1] This cottage was the quarters of Queen Morongoe.[2] Of the King's ten wives, Morongoe was his favorite.

King Sefubeng was so beloved that people said he was descended from the gods. As proof, they pointed to the birthmark on his chest. This birthmark was shaped like the moon and gave forth a beautiful golden light.

Each time a wife of the king became heavy with child, there was great rejoicing. Mouse rejoiced too. She loved motherhood. She was especially glad when Morongoe became pregnant. She loved Morongoe, who left crumbs in secret corners just for her.

Even though Morongoe was the King's favorite wife, it was not certain that her child would take over the throne. The king **decreed** that only the baby born with the moon-shaped birthmark would be his **heir.**

As it happened, the other wives gave birth before Morongoe—and all had sons. But not one of the sons had a birthmark.

Then came Morongoe's turn to give birth. Latifa,[3] the king's second favorite wife, came to help. To Morongoe's surprise, her son was born with the **coveted** birthmark.

But Latifa showed no happiness. She was jealous by nature. And when she saw the birthmark on the child's chest, she quickly left the cottage.

That evening, Mouse sat on the bed admiring the baby while Morongoe slept. A beautiful golden light filled the room. The light shone from the baby's chest as if a full moon were rising there.

Suddenly someone entered the room. Mouse saw that it was Latifa's nursemaid.[4] Silently the nursemaid slipped in and took Morongoe's baby. In the baby's place the nursemaid left a monkey.

Mouse followed the woman into the night. As she trailed

[1] (ku hu´ dē se fu´ bing) Khoedi-Sefubeng means "moon-in-chest."
[2] (mōr ong´ gō ē)
[3] (la tē´ fa)
[4] A nursemaid is a person who helps take care of a newborn baby.

the nursemaid, Mouse called friends to help her. They saw the woman enter a stable.

The animals peeked into the stable as the woman put the baby on the floor. "Wait right here, little one," she said. "I'll be right back. I just need to find a knife."

Was she going to kill the child? Quickly Mouse and her friends picked up the baby and carried it away.

"What should we do with the Moon Prince?" one mouse asked.

"We must keep him hidden," replied another.

"Take him to the cow pasture," ordered Mouse. "Surely there is a cow that can feed him milk until we can return the baby to Morongoe."

Mouse returned to Morongoe's cottage at dawn, just as the king arrived. He had come to see the infant. Of course, he wanted to know if his youngest son carried the birthmark.

But behind the king came Latifa. And before Morongoe could share the good news, Latifa lifted the wraps from around the monkey.

"Morongoe makes a **mockery** of your throne," Latifa shouted. "Look! She didn't even give birth to a human child."

Bewildered and embarrassed, the King **banished** Morongoe from his grounds. "And take this ugly monkey with you!" he ordered.

Latifa saw to it that the whole kingdom heard about Morongoe's "monkey" child. And shortly thereafter, the son of Latifa was named heir to the throne. As for Latifa—she became Queen Latifa.

Poor Morongoe was forced to leave the kingdom altogether. She left not knowing if her son was alive or dead. But in her son's place, she carried the monkey on her shoulder. No one knew where she went.

Meanwhile, Mouse spent the next several months watching over the Moon Prince. She had found a stable where he could be kept warm and dry. The cows gave him milk to drink.

But one evening Latifa happened to pass by. When she saw moonlight coming from inside the stable, she immediately knew who was inside.

"I thought you were dead!" Latifa hissed. "Well, you soon will be!"

Ever watchful, Mouse heard Latifa. And as Latifa reached to pick up the child, Mouse ran across the woman's feet. Latifa shrieked and fled.

Mouse knew that Latifa would be back. So she led the boy to a haystack. Then Mouse sent out word that she needed help.

A relative who lived in the marketplace returned with good news. "An ironsmith[5] there seeks a young **apprentice,**" the messenger said. "Perhaps he'll take the boy in."

Away they went through the night. The ironsmith was surprised to see a boy at his door. But when he saw the birthmark, he knew the child's true identity. "Come in," he said. "You'll be safe with me."

And so he was. Years passed and the boy grew into a handsome young man. The boy loved the ironsmith and learned much from him. But he felt incomplete, as if he were missing something.

Then one day the ironsmith took the young man aside. "You probably know by now that I'm not your father," the ironsmith began. "I can tell you who I think your father is."

Then the ironsmith told the prince about the king's birthmark and his mother's banishment. He also told him of Queen Latifa. "I have never trusted her," the ironsmith said. "Her son became heir to the throne too soon after your mother's banishment."

From that day on, the prince longed for the day when he could let the world know who he really was. He wanted to meet King Sefubeng and reveal the birthmark on his chest. As it was, the prince had to keep his birthmark hidden for fear that Latifa might learn of his whereabouts.

One day Mouse heard that King Sefubeng was to visit the ironsmith. It seemed that the king needed a special set of knives that only the ironsmith could produce. The ironsmith was flattered by the royal visit. But he was concerned about

---

[5] An ironsmith is a person who makes useful objects out of iron.

the prince as well.

"Stay hidden in the closet," he told the boy. "Latifa wouldn't be pleased to hear that you're still alive. Keep your robe on to hide your moonlight. It's best this way."

The prince agreed, but he hated having to hide. "I'm a man," he told himself aloud. "Men don't hide. Men defend what is theirs."

On the morning of the king's visit, the marketplace was especially busy. Vendors set out their best goods in their stalls. Others fought for spots along the king's route. One woman in a headwrap and shawl sat near the ironsmith's door. Despite the orders of the king's men, she wouldn't leave.

"Let her alone," the ironsmith said. "She hasn't done anything wrong."

Mouse sat with the prince in the closet. They watched the festivities through a large crack in the closet door. Soon they heard drums and shouts. The king was coming.

Mouse saw that Queen Latifa sat outside in her royal carriage. When King Sefubeng entered the shop, the ironsmith fell to his knees in honor of the king. Then the king and the ironsmith got down to business.

When they were finished, the king turned to go. Out of the corner of his eye, he saw golden light shining through the crack in the closet. "What light shines from inside that closet?" he asked. "It looks like moonlight."

Upon hearing the king's question, the prince pushed open the door. Then with a majestic motion, he pulled his robe away from his chest. "I'm the true heir to the throne," the Moon Prince shouted. "I carry your birthmark. I'm your son, and my mother is Morongoe."

At that moment, the woman in the headwrap burst through the door. Of course, it was Morongoe.

When she saw her son, she cried aloud. "I always believed you were alive, and here you are!" Then she turned to the astonished king. "At last I can tell you my side of the story."

When she finished, the king had Latifa imprisoned. He welcomed the Moon Prince and Morongoe back into the palace.

The Moon Prince accepted the invitation to live with his father. But Morongoe declined. She said she was happier being with humble, common people. That is where she stayed. And Mouse and the monkey stayed with her.

INSIGHTS

The homeland of the Sotho people is in southern Africa. The Sotho are the descendants of one of the Bantu groups who migrated from the Congo region nearly 2,000 years ago.

The Sotho tell many epic tales about heroes like the Moon Prince. As in this story, something unusual happened at the hero's birth. Because of his unusual birth, people knew he was special. But the hero had to face many dangers before he became king.

These epics traveled with the Sotho when they left the Congo. People called "rememberers" memorized the long stories so they would not be forgotten during the journey to the south.

Like many Bantu groups, the traditional Sotho measure a family's wealth by the amount of cattle it owns. A man usually gives his bride's family at least 15 head of cattle. Men raise the cattle and clear land for crops while women do the farming.

POINT OF VIEW

VOCABULARY PREVIEW

Below is a list of words that appear in the story. Read the list and get to know the words before you read the story.

bellowing—roaring
perspective—point of view; way of seeing
structure—shape; design

Main Characters

First man
Second man

This story ends with a question. Which of the two men was right? It's all in how you look at things.

oint of View

Inspired by a tale of the Mende people

It has been said that a mountain to an ant is but a pebble to a giraffe. In other words, how things appear depends upon your **perspective.**

This is as true with people as it is with animals.

There once were two men going to market when it became dark.

"Day is ending, for the sun sets," said one.

"Oh no," said the other. "Night begins, for the moon rises."

The two men began to argue. Which man was right?

Still arguing, the men searched for lodging.

Soon they found a room for the night and prepared for bed.

One man said, "We must sleep at the foot of the bed. That way we'll face east when morning comes."

"Then that part of the bed becomes the head," said the other.

"You're stupid," cried the first man, pointing to one end of the bed. "Look at the **structure** of the bed. See the head of the bed?" He pointed to another end. "See the foot of the bed?"

"There is no head, nor is there a foot," said the other. "A head has eyes and a nose and a mouth. A foot has a heel and toes. A bed has none of these things."

So the men argued back and forth. Which man was right?

(If you must know, they both ended up sleeping on the floor.)

In the middle of the night, one man began to snore. The other man began to walk in his sleep. The sleepwalker dreamed he was off on a great mission. Then he tripped over his companion.

The snorer dreamed he was being chased by a **bellowing** elephant. He let out a loud snore. Both men awoke at the same time.

The snorer looked at the sleepwalker standing over him. The sleepwalker looked at the snorer with his mouth still open.

"You woke me up with your sleepwalking," the snorer said.

"No, you woke me up with your snoring," the sleepwalker said.

They fussed until daylight came.

Then one man said night was gone because the sun was up. The other man said day was here because the moon had set.

And so they fussed some more.

Which man was right?

Does it matter?

INSIGHTS

Dilemma stories such as "Point of View" are told all over Africa. Here is another example from Togo in western Africa.

A man sent his three sons on a journey. After a year, each son had found one gift for his father. Before returning home, the sons met to share their findings.

The youngest son had a mirror that let the viewer see all over the country. The second son had sandals that took the wearer anyplace in the country with just one step. The eldest carried a gourd full of medicine.

The sons looked in the magic mirror to see how their father was doing. They saw that he was dead and already buried. They used the magic sandals to rush to the father's grave. Then the eldest poured his medicine onto the grave. The result? Their father came back to life.

Now which of the sons' gifts helped the father the most?